RUN TO THE FINISH

RUN TO THE FINISH

THE EVERYDAY RUNNER'S GUIDE TO AVOIDING INJURY, IGNORING THE CLOCK, AND LOVING THE RUN

AMANDA BROOKS

hachette
BOOKS

New York

Hachette Go, an imprint of Hachette Books
Hachette Book Group
1290 Avenue of the Americas, New York, NY 10104
www.HachetteGo.com
Facebook.com/HachetteGo
Instagram.com/HachetteGo

First Edition: March 2020

Hachette Books is a division of Hachette Book Group, Inc.

The Hachette Go and Hachette Books name and logos are trademarks of Hachette Book Group, Inc.

The publisher is not responsible for websites (or their content) that are not owned by the publisher.

Print book interior design by Amy Quinn.

Library of Congress Cataloging-in-Publication Data
Names: Brooks, Amanda (Runner), author.
Title: Run to the finish: the everyday runner's guide to avoiding injury, ignoring the clock, and loving the run / Amanda Brooks.
Description: First edition. | New York: Lifelong Books, 2020. | Includes bibliographical references and index.
Identifiers: LCCN 2019043017 | ISBN 9780738285993 (paperback) | ISBN 9780738286006 (ebook)
Subjects: LCSH: Running—Training. | Running—Physiological aspects. | Runners (Sports).
Classification: LCC GV1061.5 .B775 2020 | DDC 613.7/172—dc23
LC record available at https://lccn.loc.gov/2019043017
ISBNs: 978-0-7382-8599-3 (trade paperback); 978-0-7382-8600-6 (ebook)

Printed in the United States of America

LSC-C

10 9 8 7 6 5 4 3 2 1

CONTENTS

INTRODUCTION

This book is not for the elite runners. It's for me and for you and for the 98 percent of us in the middle of the pack to know that it's just fine to be the best runner you can be while juggling work, family, friends, and still enjoying that delicious slice of pizza every Friday night.

This book is for the runners who often shy away from calling themselves a runner. This book is for the runners who love the sport, but who have more to learn. This book is for the runners who aren't in it for the podium, but instead for the feeling of satisfaction from a mile well run.

It's not about dissuading you from dreaming big or setting goals for that sparkly new personal record feeling. Here, we're learning that we're more alike than we are different and why our very middle of the pack running makes us so spectacular and doesn't excuse us from learning how to train smarter.

"Forward is a pace" is the very simple motto that helped me push myself just a tad farther each day as I returned to running after an unexpected knee surgery in 2017. The previous seventeen years of building my identity as a runner needed to be reshaped, not for the first time and certainly not for the last, as I plan to continue this journey for many more decades.

Instead of lamenting where I wasn't, those four little words reminded me that every step was a success. It gave me the opportunity to embrace being a beginner once again, where my only real goal was finding a way forward each day and celebrating with fresh eyes those milestones I'd forgotten over the years. A mile was still spectacular and the day I squeaked my way back to a sub-two-hour half marathon felt just as momentous as many faster races in the past.

Forward is a pace and with that mental shift we can encourage ourselves to run to the finish of every big hairy scary goal from a 5K to a marathon to life.

A QUICK INTRODUCTION

I feel that now is a good time to tell you a few important things about myself. In case we haven't met yet or you haven't stumbled across RunToTheFinish.com while Googling a running question, that's me, Amanda Brooks.

First and possibly most important, that knee surgery was the result of a very good afternoon spent at a trampoline park.* It was not the result of being a runner. *Whew*, I'm glad we cleared that up right now and I'll talk more about our knees later in the book so we can put that long-standing myth behind us for good.

People who meet me often assume I've been a runner all my life and that, based on my ridiculous 33-inch inseam, these legs are fast. So, let's start there. Starting at age five, I played sports from softball to volleyball to swim team, but running was punishment. You know, the "you're late

---

* As a long-distance runner since 2001, I've had my share of little issues stemming from weak hips and glutes. But I had been running for nearly a decade without any major mishaps, when one day I woke to find I could no longer fully extend my left leg. This dragged on for nine months before we finally opted to do exploratory surgery, when a lot of bits and pieces, such as my meniscus and frayed cartilage, were cleaned up and my kneecap was realigned. I'm now terrified of jumping on a trampoline, but not of running.

to practice so go run laps" kind of thing that made you dread every single step and swear you'd never run again.

I vividly remember a few volleyball afternoons of grabbing my knee and dramatically limping to the sideline to get out of running. That's embarrassing now, especially when I consider the months where I pretended not to have knee pain to keep running, but a teen I was just proud of my acting skills (being an actress was my fallback plan to being a writer).

Now, for the fast part. While *fast* is relative, generally my motto is, I run far, not fast. Although I have scrambled onto a few podiums, even after eight marathons and 21,000 miles running, I'm not yet a Boston Qualifier, I'm not an-easy-run-at-a-seven-minute-pace runner, and I'm not a went-out-for-a-short-20-miler-over-lunch runner. Which is why I feel qualified to discuss life in the middle of the pack. I may have done thousands of hours of research and coaching, but my miles are largely spent in the company of most other runners who are also on the largest part of the bell curve.

Next up, there tends to be a common assumption that I'm a perfectionist. I was, after all, a straight-A student and even graduated magna cum laude from the University of Missouri. Honestly, school was easy for me and I just did the required work. Which is to say that had it been hard, I would have tried and put forth effort, but I'm not the person who would have belabored every detail to go from a B to an A (though I am the person who will always have a project done a week early).

In my world, perfect is a tremendous waste of mental energy because someone is always going to find ways you could have done it better. This isn't to say that I settle for less than my best or I'm okay with mediocrity. But it is to say that I believe good solid hard work is enough to allow you to enjoy the ride with a whole lot less stress, and that's a lifestyle I can stand behind happily. Which means if you see a misplaced comma, I hope you'll focus on the bigger message and not the error.

Finally, you need to know that I'm a student of running. I've written over two thousand highly researched articles on running; I devour every running book that comes out; I pick the brains of every coach, sports medicine doctor, or physical therapist that I come in contact with, to help ensure that I'm always sharing the best information. I love this sport deep down to my core and my greatest wish is for us all to run healthy and happy for as many years as possible.

In other words, I hope we can run to the finish together.

13.1 SIGNS YOU'RE A RUNNER

1. You own more running shoes than regular shoes (okay, more running shoes than shoes owned by the rest of your family).

2. Your running gear costs more than the rest of your wardrobe (and you don't even care).

3. You can't wait for vacation because it means extra time to run (and often new places to run).

4. You understand words like *fartlek*, *pronation*, and Pose Method (and you love to talk about them).

5. You wake up earlier on Saturday to run than for work on Monday (and you don't even mind).

6. You can complain about the pain of running and extol its virtues in the same sentence ("That pain made me a better person").

7. You often find yourself assuming anyone who passes you isn't running as far (they couldn't possibly be; you're a distance runner!).

8. You have ridiculous tan lines and are proud of them because they represent hard work (and, yes, even with sunscreen you get them).

9. You know that peanut butter is a valid food group and best eaten on a slice of bread with banana before a race.

10. You know it's not weird to run back and forth in front of your house to get to round numbers. (Only psychos leave things at 4.27.)

11. You're convinced running solves nearly all life problems (because you are extremely smart).

12. You have solved world hunger and other life-altering things during a run (you just can't remember them later).

13. You await Marathon Monday as others do the Super Bowl (and you're ridiculously unproductive at work watching it).

13.1 You know life is better when you run. It doesn't matter how far, it doesn't matter how fast, it doesn't matter if it's solo or with friends. Any mile is a good mile.

CHAPTER 1

YOU ARE A RUNNER

The majority of us fall squarely in the middle of the pack

We don't make the news or viral videos.

We don't get special accolades.

We don't leave others in awe.

It's time to celebrate our averageness. Did you know you can exhibit manliness, graciousness, awkwardness, cheerfulness, or even weakness, but averageness is simply not a word? As though being in the middle leaves you unnoticed and undervalued? Why don't we celebrate those in the middle? After all, we're the majority.

We're squarely in the middle.

Vanilla.

Average.

Forgotten.

Only, we aren't truly forgotten. We're the biggest part of the running population and it's time to embrace the way that it makes you more alike than different from your running peers. It's time to let go of feeling like you need to run a certain pace to be recognized. It's time to be free of the worries about what others think when you choose not to run a marathon. It's our time to run because we choose to.

Who's really judging your runs? That inner voice whispering it's too hard for you? The horrific timed mile of childhood that made you feel ashamed of moving too slow? The softball coach who mocked your awkward stride as you grew?

Or is the judge you? When you look at runners you admire with their postrace PR (personal record) glow and huge grins biting into their most recent race medal, à la an Olympian, how does it make you feel? Do you despair at the gap between the current numbers on your Garmin and how you'd like to run?

That inner voice questioning your goals might tag along for the entirety of your life or, with some grace and luck, running might be the tool to help you leave it behind. In fact, while logging those miles, you might begin to see it's popping up as a defense mechanism. A bad one, mind you, but perhaps that voice is an attempt to protect you—from rejection, from failure, from disappointment.

When your inner Simon Cowell begins to rear his ugly head again, it's time to redirect. Running is a mental sport and this is the moment when you choose to become a stronger runner even if that means never subtracting a single second from your race time. It's the moment when you realize showing up, trying, enjoying the run, laughing with friends . . . all of that matters just as much as the clock ever will.

As Epicurus so profoundly said, "Do not spoil what you have by desiring what you have not; remember that what you now have was once among the things you only hoped for." Too many of us are unhappy with our running. If you want to run, run. And let this book be your guide to the tactics that will make you a better runner, a stronger runner, and an injury-free runner who is motivated by the joy and not the fear.*

---

* If you're like, "No, really and truly, my heart's deepest desire is to be fast and Boston Qualify," that's absolutely fine, too! You simply need to be prepared to embrace all the things those fast runners do. It's not missing runs, it's superfocused nutrition, it's the strength work, the stretching, and a lot of the things that we will talk about here, but you're gonna have to take it to another level.

MEET MARGIE

Step one in our You Are a Runner Program is to accept that you have some mental programming that needs reworking. Although the words might be unique to you, it's a part of running that everyone from the first finisher to the last must learn to battle.

I'm not sure how Margie got her name, but likely after a solid long run of muttering, "You will not win, asshat," I decided my inner critic should have a name. Also, realizing that people might assume I was on a phone call with my wireless ear buds if I said "Margie" instead of "asshat," made it seem like another brilliant idea birthed while on the run.

Margie sounds like someone I shouldn't take all that seriously, which is exactly what I wanted. She's large Marge from *Pee-wee's Playhouse* or perhaps the newer version, that I may or may not watch on a certain *Real Housewives* show while on the treadmill, with platinum blond pigtails and sequins.

We've all got an inner Margie. I'd love to say Margie is there to protect you, but Margie is there to protect your ego. And her way of doing that is by replaying all the bad runs, the crappy coaches, and the experiences that have ever told you that you aren't an athlete.

Yes, I said "athlete." I'm not sure why runners refuse to accept that they're athletes, but you are. Athletes show up to training day after day. You show up for your runs day after day. Athletes plan their workouts and find a way to make it all happen. You juggle life around training with miraculous dexterity. Athletes spend time taking care of their body. You spend time foam rolling, stretching, and I'm sure, getting monthly massages, right?

When she begins reminding me that each time I pick up the pace, I begin huffing like a longtime smoker or that I might injure myself, I can give her a little side eye and pretend she doesn't know squat. Which in fact is true, but there's something important that happens when we're willing to bring our fears to the light. We can face them to truly see whether they're valid or simply a ghost story we've let take on too much reality.

What Margie neglects to include in her angry diatribe about your shortcomings, is all the work you've done since that painstaking timed mile to get stronger, healthier, and mentally tougher. It might sound a little crazy—you're a runner, so you get crazy—but you need to start having regular conversations with her.

Talking to yourself isn't that weird. We have all walked into a room and said to no one, *"What was I looking for?"* This time, you're simply having a conversation with your subconscious. Right now, Margie is running the show because you try to ignore her or you let her win by accepting her words as truth, rather than as a story.

For example, a typical run with Margie:

> Margie: You can't hold this pace, what are you trying to do?
> You: Gahh, you're right, I'm going to burn out before I can finish.
> Margie: That's because you just aren't a fast runner.

You may be thinking, "Well, Margie is right," and already replaying her words, *"I need to accept the fact that I'm just not going to get faster,"* and I'm here to say, "Hogwash." Margie doesn't know what you're capable of achieving; she's not there to pump you up; rather, to pump the breaks and keep you in a nice, safe place. You, however, have graduated to adulting and are fully capable of protecting yourself and replacing the toilet paper roll.

Taking control of your thoughts results in a conversation more like this:

> Margie: Why are you trying to push so hard? You're never going to win the race anyway.
> You: Thank you for the input. I'm enjoying seeing what I can do.
> Margie: But you're going to get hurt.
> You: Again, thank you for the concern, but I've trained for this.

Morgan Freeman: And she would then continue to run for another three miles with a smile.

Notice, I'm not trying to get you to *Secret* yourself out of this by envisioning a gold medal performance. Instead, we're acknowledging our fear and then continuing on with the run because we love doing this, and why shouldn't we spend our time enjoying the miles, rather than fretting about the numbers on a watch?

Once you've acknowledged the thoughts, it's time to start reciting your mantra and shut her down entirely. Your brain works incredibly fast processing the approaching car, the barking dog, and of course the pace on that watch. It doesn't have time for you to also recognize the subconscious beliefs Margie is not so subtly shouting: "*This is too hard for me,*" "*I'm probably tired after a week of long work hours,*" and "*Maybe this was all a bad idea.*"

Which means it's *your* job to give your subconscious *new* programming. Better thoughts mean better runs. Better runs means sticking to it a lot longer. Sticking to it longer means getting the results you've been chasing.

One of the fastest ways to start reprogramming is to select a mantra that resonates with you. Each time you repeat it, your brain and body respond. The more you use it, the more it becomes so ingrained that you'll start thinking it by default, which gives Margie less opportunity to voice her unwanted opinions.

My personal favorite: *Stronger and stronger with every mile.* Imagine the feeling that puts into your legs and the smile on your face, as you begin repeating in your mind over and over that you actually feel better the farther you go. Your body will respond to these thoughts just as easily as the thoughts that it's too hard and you need to stop.

If distance isn't your goal, then start testing out other ideas:

- It feels good when my legs run faster.
- My breathing is light and easy.
- Every step brings me closer to my goal.

- I feel alive.
- Light, quick, and free.
- I eat hills for breakfast. (Of course, they're hard; why not embrace it!)

Elite runner Amy Hastings has a great one, which helped her win a number of championships by staying focused on the positive: *I breathe in strength. I breathe out weakness.* Kara Goucher wrote an entire book around her mantra of *Strong* and how the process of defining a new mantra for each big running goal helped her to remain focused. Take advantage of their access to sports psychologists who have proven how valuable this is, and do it yourself for free.

Simply by choosing to run, you've already set yourself apart from the masses. That being the case, I want to talk a little more about this idea of how we see ourselves and how we define our running in the middle of the pack. Because even the greatest mantra can't work its magic if you're holding on to outdated ideas.

BUT I'M NOT A REAL RUNNER

Let's deal with "real runner" syndrome right now. It's an epidemic currently afflicting 1 in every 4 runners, based on my unscientific poll of one hundred runners. Kidding; I clearly polled 32.2 runners.

This is one of the most common discussions I have with new and even longtime runners who hold an outdated idea of themselves. I know you think it's easy for me, with seventeen-plus years of running, to say we're all real runners, but the truth is that I had to get there the same way as you, by adjusting my mind-set one footstep at a time.

For me, it all started with a hill. Just one superlong foreboding hill that made me believe I was a walker who occasionally sped up to what looked like a run.* After months of making the same loop from my

---

* Unless you looked at photos and then it still appeared to be a walk, which is one of the most unfortunate things about race photos. I swear I'm running, they swear I'm walking, and we both agree the angle is without fail unflattering.

college apartment, over and over, I decided just to run a little way up *the* hill. Not the whole way; that sounded insane. I could quit at any time, I mean I wasn't a real runner, so it didn't matter if I stopped. I was just a girl who sometimes ran, but mostly walked.

This isn't a story of triumph. I absolutely quit halfway up that mile-long incline. But I also had a grin I couldn't contain because my endorphins were starting to help me realize, *"Hey, I made it halfway."* Me, the not a real runner.

In fact, I was only attempting to run up that hill because some friends were going to do the 2002 Nashville Rock n Roll Half Marathon. A road trip sounded fun. Bonding with friends sounded cool. Running was an afterthought.

The run-walk method became my initial strategy as a college student, simply because that's what I could do. I had no actual training plan and didn't understand the concept of the Galloway method (see Chapter 6), so I ran until I was too tired to keep running and then I walked. Nonetheless, my twenty-year-old body handled it like a champ and I built up to a 10-mile-long run before race day.

But I was never a runner. You know those lithe, speedy-looking people who make running appear effortless, interesting, and well . . . fun.* I just knew that a "real runner" would never walk on race day and I wasn't sure how I could possibly do 13.1 miles without walking. Although that became a driving goal that would push me on many runs.

I finished that first race in 2:17 with burning legs and lungs, and a brain that was thoroughly trashed from not having a lick of fuel or hydration. While I was collecting my banana, I turned to catch the elite marathon runners starting to come through. Brain explosion; they'd run twice as far in the same time!

Obviously, I wore my medal everywhere the next day, but I still kept the whole thing pretty low key because I didn't yet fully understand the magnitude of the choices I'd just made. Racing wasn't what hooked me on running, and even 21,000 miles later, it's not what defines me as a

---

* Sorry to everyone who'd like to punch me, as I'm told that I now appear to be that person. Also, I'm happy to send you plenty of bad race photos to prove it wasn't always so.

runner. But soon after, something happened to switch my mind-set on the whole concept of being a real runner.

HOW TO FEEL LIKE A REAL RUNNER

For me, the defining moment had nothing to do with pace or even a race, and everything to do with a *why*. I wasn't running because it was required by a coach for being late or even as an excuse to road trip with friends. I was running solely because I wanted to. I was choosing the hard thing for no other reason than I could.

The truth is, the day you take your first step toward running, voluntarily or not, you are in fact a runner. But that's not the same thing as *feeling* like a runner. Something magic happens when you accept the label. Runner. Athlete. Rock star.

If you aren't there yet, it's time to embrace the long-practiced art of faking it 'til you make it. I mean, imagine what you'd do differently if you were a real runner and not just someone who jogs for fun or needs walk breaks. By acting as if you're already a real runner, you will start to shift your patterns just a bit.

Might you warm up before runs?

Spend time on the wonderfully painful foam roller?

Think more about your postrun nutrition?

Buy the shoe that fits your foot and not the shoe size you've always been?

Show up to a group run because you know it will push you?

Sign up to work with a coach because you want to stay injury-free and progress?

Walk into a running store with confidence?

None of these are Earth-shattering choices, but they are subtle shifts in your mentality about how you treat your runs and your body.

In fact, maybe as a real runner, you'd still have some terrible, horrible, no good, very bad runs. I sure do! But, instead of scolding yourself and using it to prove your nonrunner thought process, you'd see what there was to learn from that run. Have you been increasing your mileage or working out more, so your body needs time to adapt? Have you been up late all week building a magnificent papier-mâché volcano? Have you been eating the M&M's off your co-worker's desk instead of taking time for lunch?

What I want you to know is that feeling like a real runner won't happen the day you hit a certain pace or complete a specific distance. Those are goals to get you started and that might motivate you to show up on days when you'd rather sleep in. But the glorious moment that you decide you are a runner is like watching the sky turn a brilliant orange over the horizon as the sun peeks out to warm your face.

Every run takes on a new meaning and becomes an opportunity to change your life in remarkable ways.

Now that I have waxed poetic about my love for this sport, though, yes, it took me a good couple of years to own that title myself, let's get to the concrete action plan:

1. Put on your shoes.
2. Go for a run; the pace doesn't matter.
3. Celebrate every little victory from a new distance to less walk breaks to no pain.
4. Repeat. Repeat. Repeat.

Today, right now, you have been dubbed a real runner and henceforth you shall be known as Fleetfoot. Okay, I see it would be weird to have thousands of readers using the same name, so let's just go with last names, plus the most recent animal you passed on a run. Nice to meet you; I'm Brooks Coyote.

You have now joined a club, virtual or real, that accepts you because you take action whether you're stick thin, carrying some baby weight, speedy like the Road Runner, or waddling like Daffy Duck. You are far more alike than different and every time you choose to show up, you inspire someone else just like you to do the same.

STANDARD NOT-A-REAL-RUNNER ISSUES

I know we're all special and therefore our personal reasons for feeling like not a real runner, probably mean it's true, right? Here are a few of the most common e-mails I receive:

WHAT IF I RUN ON THE TREADMILL?

Ah yes, what is often referred to as the dreadmill has many runners believing that their choice to use it, instead of being hard-core about the weather, the dark, the fact that they don't want to push a triple jogging stroller, makes them less of a runner.

No, no, my friend. This is faulty logic. Many extremely fast and accomplished runners use the treadmill. It's a fantastic tool for staying safe, for varying your terrain when it's not readily available, and yes, the softer surface often helps many runners keep going longer.*

WHAT IF I NEED TO WALK?

Walk your heart out. I wish more runners had the benefit of a few hardcore trails in their life, when suddenly they realize that walking isn't a negative, it's a conservation of energy to ensure they can finish the distance. Ultrarunners use walking to their benefit, as a way to finish races faster because they didn't overexert themselves forcing a run on the steep uphills.

Of course, walking is technically a different action than running, but using walk breaks to extend your distance or to recover from hard intervals is just smart training.

WHAT IF I CAN'T BEAT OPRAH?

I'm always amused when people tell me their only goal for a first marathon is to beat Oprah Winfrey's time.

It's not like we're talking about sixty-year-old Oprah who prefers to spend her days in the garden. She was quite fit at that point, age forty in

---

* My personal treadmill has over 14,000 miles on it and I am for sure a real runner. I have a laminated card to prove it.

1994, and completed the Marine Corps Marathon in 4:29. That's a darn fine first marathon time. Mine was 4:17, so I guess I win the beat Oprah prize. Do I get a shirt? And is it wicking?

Oprah herself accidentally started this trend by saying, "If I can do it, anyone can do it." That simple statement inspired many of her followers to begin running and then slowly morphed into a different mind-set: "*I just want to beat Oprah's time.*"

Finishing a marathon puts you in very elite company (less than 1% of the population). Being surrounded by runners, we often think it's not such a big deal, but the majority of people have never and will never run 26.2. Your first marathon should be about enjoying the experience, embracing the insane milestones, and realizing just what you're capable of achieving.

Again, it's not about the clock. Finishing a marathon is a massive achievement and quite honestly even more so when you've spent seven hours on the course. That takes mental and physical stamina beyond most people's comprehension.

WHAT IF I DON'T LOOK LIKE A RUNNER?

Head out to a race start line. Examine the variety of sizes, shapes, genders, and ethnicities that you see. The front might well be packed with very slim, tiny-shorts-wearing runners, but as you continue to look around, you'll see a smorgasbord of bodies.

Want runners to look like you? Show up. Join the community. Help others feel comfortable doing the same. Remember, at one point, Kathrine Switzer didn't look like society's definition of a runner. And Ashley Graham wasn't a traditional model. But they showed up and opened doors for others to do what they love, just as they are.

If you're worried about being judged, that's okay. We're all nervous the first time we show up to any new group. Luckily 97 percent* of runners I've encountered in person, online, and around the world are thrilled

---

* The other 3 percent were probably friends with Margie and we already know I don't think her opinion counts.

to welcome someone new to the club. Honestly, we're giddy at the idea of a new runner because we have someone else who will talk running with us incessantly.

WHAT IF I HAVEN'T RUN IN A WHILE? LIKE, A REALLY LONG WHILE?

Maybe you ran cross-country in high school and then took an extended break to adulthood; maybe you had kids and time just seemed to vanish; maybe you've been injured and the comeback feels never-ending.

None of that precludes you from the club. Decide that this is the week you're going to dust off your shoes (or maybe buy new ones for extra motivation and to ensure the cushion hasn't dissolved from disuse) and head out. Leave your expectations at the door and remember what it's like to move your body. Congrats; you're a runner again.

WHAT IF I DON'T WANT ANYONE TO SEE ME?

In college, I often found myself sweating in the living room to the energetic words of Billy Blanks Tae Bo! I was rocking a punch, when I'd hear the jingle of keys and scramble to hit Pause, then dash to the bathroom to wash my face. I'll be darned if I was going to let my roommate see me looking like a fool.

I get it. You don't have to run with a group. You don't have to run outside. You don't have to ever sign up for a race. There's a process of gaining confidence that isn't always instant. But here's the thing: most of us don't look like the gazelles at the front of the pack. And yet when people see us running as they motor on by, the majority are thinking, "Good for them" or "I should really exercise." Like the previous point, you just never know who you might inspire to get out and improve their own health by showing that you're taking charge of yours.

Additionally, I will say you're missing out on a big part of what makes running a truly different sport than any other. We get to show up on the same playing field as the best there is. Our times might be slower, but we complete the exact same distance, on the exact same course, with all the fans along the way cheering for our effort.

WHAT IF I DON'T WANT TO RUN A HALF MARATHON OR MARATHON?

I know these races get the glory. They're the only ones televised, the only ones that seem to attract celebrity attention, and we do make a gigantic fuss over anyone finishing 26.2 miles because it's a pretty insane achievement.

But a fast 5K can be a great deal harder than 26.2, which is in fact why I stand by my statement that I run far, not fast. Showing up in spite of nerves to run any distance is an achievement. If pace isn't what makes you a real runner, neither is distance.

WHAT IF I DON'T WANT TO RACE AT ALL?

Welcome to my world. I love running for me. In fact, I stopped training for marathons for a few years because I felt that I was losing the joy of the sport and that, to me, wasn't worth any medal, no matter the size, shape, spinner, or bling.

Races are a fantastic way to connect with other runners, reinvigorate your desire to push hard thanks to the atmosphere, and test yourself. But they certainly aren't what make you a runner. If you have no issues getting out the door (or to the treadmill) every week without a race on the line, then don't feel pressured to sign up. Enjoy your miles, however you want.

WHAT IF I JUST HATE RUNNING?

I'll be honest; I'm not 100 percent certain why you picked up this book, but I'm going to assume that it's because somewhere deep inside you want to enjoy running.

First, no one has to run. It's not the only way to lose weight. It's not the only way to get fit. It's not required for the majority of jobs.

Second, I hated running when my coach was yelling at me as I followed that blue line around and around the hardwood floors. I hated it more when I had to run from one line to the other in an aptly named suicide drill. Maybe you, too, just need an opportunity to run without the pressure.

I suppose that even if you just loathe it to your core, but you do it, you are a runner. I can only hope you find something in here to help your heart grow just a few sizes and not to troll me later on Instagram. Thanks!

DON'T BE A JOGGER—IT'S A COP-OUT FOR NOT A REAL RUNNER

Jogger.

There it is again, that word. *Shudder.*

The talented Haruki Murakami, in *What I Talk About When I Talk About Running*, refers to passing fellow joggers quite early in his book, and in England, *joggers* are the shoes worn for running. Clearly, it's not a derogatory term, so what's my beef?

We don't call them elite joggers or marathon joggers, they're runners. Yet, every news headline that involves a runner uses the term *jogger*. Why does the news so love this term? Jogger finds dead body. Jogger abducted while running. Jogger wins the lottery. I graduated from the top journalism school in the United States and can say with certainty there was no course where we learned that anyone moving faster than a walk should be called a jogger. I don't remember all the rules around commas, but this I got.

Maybe it's a holdover from the era where runners were the elite few who ran marathons and everyone else was a red velour tracksuit shuffling around the block while hoping their neighbors didn't see them jogging. Racing was for a select few and everyone else was just playing at the sport.

What I'm trying to say is that sometimes labels matter. Most often I hear it from fellow runners to denigrate what they do: "*No, no, I just jog sometimes.*" It's the easiest way to say you aren't a real runner.

If that takes some pressure off your runs, allowing you to head out and enjoy it more freely, then I'll give you a pass. But if you're doing it to diminish yourself because of the clock, then it's gotta stop. Just because our focus isn't on breaking the finish line tape doesn't make the time spent pounding the roads less valuable. And what would races be without the 99 percent of us who aren't in the elite pack?

A race without us would simply be a small group of very fit, very fast people racing for medals. We call that the Olympics, and as you might notice, it only happens once every four years. Of course, there's a whole boatload of pride involved in their wins, but I venture to say it's not the same as when I finally stopped pretending that I had knee pain and found myself instead victoriously running all the way up my nemesis hill.

The middle is where we fall in love with the process, the triumph, the grit, the attitude of determination. It's why spectators clumped around the finish line find themselves unexpectedly in tears. There's a story in every finish. The new mother blowing kisses to her baby on the side-lines, as the seventy-year-old grandfather sneaks across the line behind her with a confident smile and a little "yippee," and the inflated dinosaur runner collapses just after the timing mat because 26.2 in costume is hot as Hades.

Our sport gets less love in the media because both elites and everyday runners share the same gear, training courses, and big game day. It's over-looked in a way because running is available to everyone. We do it freely as kids, and if we're lucky, find it again as we get older.

Yet, that shared commonality is part of what draws us in. Watching elites burst across the New York City Marathon finish line, we know what it took to hold that blazing speed for 26.2 miles. We feel a little hero worship at their 120-mile training weeks, thinking how hard we work to hit our own mileage. We aren't them and aren't trying for the same goals, but we can relate. We understand the commitment; we learn from their fierce training; we respect them without putting them on a pedestal that they can't manage.

Sharing the sport might make it less exciting to televise, but for runners, it's part of the fun: recognizing that there's always more you can achieve in your runs and that, unlike in other sports, you don't need to be drafted, and you don't need a team or a manager, if you want to set your sights at the top.

What if you fell in love with the middle? What if that allowed you to enjoy running more? What if that led to training more effectively and putting in more miles? Hmmmm, that sounds like a recipe for a PR!

It's a crazy thing that by releasing some pressure, we often find ourselves running better than ever. The next time you're frustrated by lack of progress or comparing your hard workout to someone on Instagram lamenting their "slow seven-minute miles," step back. Think beyond the clock.

Consider the other ways you've shown up for yourself by committing to running. How you've improved and the ways that it's changed you both physically and mentally. While a great race or a PR can put you on cloud nine, it's really every step before that's helped reshape you. Embrace the label. It's not about a speed. It's about what it means. It's about the community you're joining and what you want from your choice to lace up.* You are a runner.

EMBRACE THE RUNNER'S NOD

If you're looking for some additional concrete steps to feel like a runner, read this. If you truly want to join the club, this is where it's at, the runner's nod.

In those first years of running, I could have told you a lot about my shoes, not because I'd yet made my way into a running store to find a decent shoe. I kept my eyes down while running because I was still battling

---

* And to any journalists who might happen to pick this up, we implore you to stop calling us joggers.

an inner idea that without hitting a certain pace, I was too slow to be considered a runner.

If I didn't make eye contact, I could pretend no one noticed me.

One day, after another battle with the hill, I looked up.

I was a runner and I wanted to own it.

I held my pride (and my breath) and there it was . . . the nod.

That passing runner probably thought nothing of it, but I knew what it meant: **I'd joined the club.** I was officially part of that select crew that acknowledged each other's efforts on the road with the subtle "I see you" of the runner's nod.

Of course, he could have given me a flick of the hand or a hello, but there's something about the nod that really feels like you've joined a secret club. A club that says we don't need to talk about this, we don't need to share a language, we might never meet again, but we both know we're out here crushing it (whether that's a speed walk or sub-six-minute mile).

Of course, there are variations on the nod, which we tend to interchange depending on the day, our speed, and yes, our mood.

- Nod + smile = I'm having a great freaking run.
- Nod - smile = I see you, I'm working too hard to be loving this yet.
- Flick of the finger = I'm going real fast, but hey.
- Wave of the hand = Wassup, this is hard.
- Good morning = this jerk is clearly not working hard enough, who can talk?! (kidding!)

The more I travel, I've found subtle differences from city to city. But I still always give the nod or the wave because I know how much it means on the receiving end. Just do it.

ADDITIONAL WAYS TO FEEL IT

Once you've embraced the nod, there are a few other things you can do to begin shifting your perspective.

Log It

Get a running log or start marking your runs on the calendar. "What we measure, we manage" is one of the best pieces of life advice I've ever received. It's exciting to watch those numbers day after day or to remind yourself of how far you've come. In time, you'll flip back to those first rough weeks and think now those are your recovery days.

Logging your miles can be as public or private as you'd like it to be. Some people find extra motivation in sharing it on Instagram or Strava; meanwhile, people like me talk about running nonstop, but log our workouts privately in a Google spreadsheet. Starting out, however, I loved the visual of seeing those numbers penned into my wall calendar. Find the method that feels best for you and get started.

Upgrade It

Head to a running store and let the staff help you find a solid pair of running shoes. Like me, you probably started out in whatever pair you had lying around. Absolutely fine. However, getting that first pair of high-quality running shoes is a game changer. Your body appreciates it and you've also just signaled to your brain again that you're a runner.

If you're nervous about the running store, put it aside. Running stores are there to help you and the salespeople know it can be intimidating, so most try to be very helpful and ready to answer your questions.

Plan It

Ever notice that marathon runners are often heard turning down Friday night invitations—"*Sorry, I can't, I've got to get up early for a long run.*" Not only have they planned it, but they're sticking to it and embracing their very runnerness.*

Start putting runs in your calendar as appointments not to miss. Tell people that you're going running or went running; you might as well let them start thinking of you as a runner, too. They'll also begin to ask

---

* Like *averageness*, this is not yet a word. I've got a whole slew of runner words, though, that I believe we can in fact popularize and make changes.

about those runs, which adds in a layer of accountability that I often hear is needed. Another unintended bonus is that most runners become more efficient at work because it's necessary to squeeze in their runs.

LEARN IT

Start reading more books about running; the one in your hand is a very good start. Start listening to podcasts about running, following runners on Instagram, checking out running magazines and blogs.

Fear is a result of the unknown. Make running more familiar and you'll immediately start to feel more comfortable and confident. Plus, listening to a podcast from Desi Linden about the mental task of winning the Boston Marathon or Bart Yasso about continuing to run despite Lyme disease, will absolutely propel you forward. A great podcast will always make me feel like, if they can survive that, maybe I can do just a little bit more. And that, my friend, is a definite real runner mind-set.

RUNCTIONARY

A definitive guide to the running words you may not know, but will enjoy adding to your vocabulary to showcase your pure love and absolute obsession with the sport. Also, useful to decipher what I'm saying.

Runch—Enjoying a run during lunch while everyone else is stuffing their face or still sitting at their desk working.

Runsploration—The pure joy of running through a new place without a planned route.

Runmarathoning—The twice-yearly moments when major marathons are televised and you can run on the treadmill while watching the race for extra motivation.

Runsplaining—The act of one runner speaking to another from a place of superiority. Your mama's right, you're special, but you aren't better. Tone it down.

Runger—Running-induced hunger. Don't get between a tired runner and their food.

Runtastic—No, not the app, just a general exclamation that something is as good as a runner's high.

Emo Legs—That moment during a race where you have to rein in your overwhelming emotions to keep your legs moving forward. Interestingly in ultramarathons, runners often collapse right before the finish because their brain sees the finish and thinks it's done.

CHAPTER 2

MOTIVATION BEYOND THE CLOCK

Now that you've accepted you are in fact a runner and your worth isn't tied to the watch, what else is there? If you aren't shooting for a PR and racing every month, is there a point to pushing yourself through long runs or speed sessions?

For some runners, the answer to that is no. They thrive on competition and it's absolutely part of what draws them to the sport. This book is not for them. This book is for people like me who want to compete with themselves, but also have an idea in their mind about how they want running to feel, how they want it to be part of their life and part of who they are.

My goal is to run for many years, not just one race. More accurately, my goal is to remain passionately in love with running until I'm old, gray, and rocking on the front porch. I never want to lose the joy of the movement, the experience of taking in the world around me, or the feeling of achievement in an effort to hit a specific time.

This is important not only for my soul and my health, but my long-standing promise that I'll Boston Qualify by age eighty. I nearly had #BQby80* trending on Instagram with so many people jumping on board and proclaiming that was absolutely how they'd like to do it, too. We need to just hang on to our current fitness, allowing the time standards to come to us, rather than the other way around.

Of course, if you hang on with me and they keep lowering the time standards, this is going to become a whole different story and I may need to knock you down in a future race with hopes that your bones are just slightly less strong than mine. I know, I said I wasn't competitive with anyone besides myself, but I think after another fifty years of running, that could change. But that's a run we'll cross when we need to.

PRIDE POWERED

What's there to remain motivated by, if not a race? For me, it often boils down to one word: *pride*. There's an immense amount of pride with every run that I finish, whether 1 mile or 26.2. Which might sound a bit ego-centric, but stick with me for a moment because I think this might just be the feeling you've been trying to pinpoint yourself.

Running is not easy. In fact, it's freaking hard a lot of days. And yet, we choose it.

There's a satisfaction in knowing that we're choosing to do the hard thing time after time and it certainly contributes to the feeling of a runner's high. Which is not the same as a Rocky Mountain high, so I've been told, but it's much more satisfying and legal in all fifty states. Instead, our endorphin high is the reward for putting in the work and testing ourselves without any requirement to do so.

---

* Feel free to start using it again! I'm on board for this crazy goal and happy to support anyone else looking to run for many years to come. If you're currently seventy-nine with a BQ, maybe just use #IAmAmazing instead.

The longer I've been running, the more I can elicit these feelings even on a bad run and the more I find that other runners can relate. They couldn't quite put their finger on what it is that keeps them going in between races, but *pride* summed it up pretty well.

Pride: a feeling of deep pleasure or satisfaction derived from one's own achievements.

Yes, that's exactly it. We often confuse pride with ego and feel weird saying we're proud of ourselves for doing a little 3-miler around the neighborhood. But, honestly, why not be just as proud of a single mile as we are of 26.2?

We all know that some days, every step feels as if an elephant is tethered to our waist with a bungie cord, and others, we seem to glide along with the energy to go extra miles. Those two aren't mutually exclusive; they're part of the running process and happen through the evolution of our consistency, intensity, and total life stress. Without getting too far off track, let's say you'll find more on that in Chapter 6, "The Perfect Training Plan."

But how can you feel the same level of pride when finishing a marathon or when having a really horrendous run that makes you question everything about your life?

You still showed up.

You still tried.

You still made progress by moving forward.

I don't consider that failure, ever, not even if you walked it in. And I bet, now that you've started to think about it, you wouldn't, either.

GOING BACK TO THAT FIRST MILE

It's so easy to take a simple mile for granted. When you first start running, it's the longest mile on Earth, but soon thereafter, you surpass that milestone and suddenly it's "just" a mile. It becomes about accumulating more miles or running those miles faster. This is where the judgment of our running begins.

Once we can run for hours on end, why should 1 mile ever be cause for celebration? We already know we can do it. But knowing you can do something and choosing to do it consistently are very different, and what if that little shift allows us to hold on to the enjoyment of running?

I recognized years ago that I was never going to be the woman consistently on top of the podium or the runner who did the most challenging races, but I was the runner who could find value in each mile. Let's just see how this mind-set might make even those no-good runs just a little bit better.

It's maddeningly frustrating when the first mile of a run feels like the last mile of a race, but learning to appreciate the effort might be the ticket to fixing it on the run. What if, when that frustration appears, instead of judging the run and comparing it to all the others that were harder or faster or longer or snowier or hotter or you name the condition that immediately makes you feel bad, what if we do something radically different?

We don't fight it.

We don't get angry at ourselves.

We take a deep breath and smile.

BECAUSE, NO MATTER WHAT, YOU'RE STILL RUNNING.

Sometimes we spend so much time trying to *push* the rock up a hill (not that your body is a rock, unless you like rocks and then it's a spectacular geode) that, if we just relax a little, we'd remember that rolling downhill is way more fun. In fact, by releasing all that tension, we're freeing up more oxygen to flow to our muscles, and by smiling, we're actually sending signals to our brain that we enjoy this.

Science has your back on this one. Smiling during a workout releases hormones that make your brain perceive the effort as less, which translates to your body feeling better. And if it just keeps sucking the life out of you, for goodness' sake, walk. One of the great pleasures of releasing the pressure for every run to be about beating your previous time is you can go fast on some days and slow on other days, all depending on what feels best.

Maybe by taking the pressure off that particular run, you're giving your body the break it needs to fully recover from the last hard run. Training plans aren't written in stone; we running coaches don't have the time to chisel them in, we're busy running ourselves.

It's easy, when injured, to wish for a single mile and easy, after a great race, to feel that you should run that way daily. The hard part is finding enjoyment in any mile, whether it's speed work, recovery, or hard as hell, but that's also where the biggest rewards are found. Kind of like the middle. All those miles in between the highs and lows are like us, worthy of being celebrated.

CULTIVATING YOUR OWN PRIDE FACTOR

Maybe *pride* isn't the word that resonates with you, but there is a feeling that drives you. I call it your why. And no race will ever propel you to show up in the freezing rain with the same level of joy as finding your why.

Personal trainer Jillian Michaels frequently talks about this concept of a deeper why.* She reminds people that getting slim for a wedding might drive you for a bit, but most people later put back on the weight they lost if they don't have a bigger why. It's the same with sticking to running for more than a check on your bucket list of experiences.

If you have kids, I find this is where they might unknowingly drag the answer out of you.

> You: Mommy needs to go run.
> Child: Why?
> You: Because I have a race coming up.

---

* She also states that she hates running and now it's become a life goal to have a long conversation with her about why we find it so amazing.

Child: Why?

  You: Because I signed up for it.

Child: Why?

  You: Because I needed a goal to keep me motivated.

Child: Why?

  You: Because getting out of this house helps me keep my sanity.

Child: Why?

  You: Because sometimes I need to feel like I'm doing things for me and all those endorphins make me happy, which helps me come home and answer all your questions without playing a game of hide-and-seek where you'd never find me, hunkered down in the tub with a sleeve of Oreos.

If you lack inquisitive children or maybe are just ready to dive in a little deeper, a few tips to find your lasting why:

- Get emotional: how do you want to feel?
- Get honest: are you doing this for you?
- Reflect: at what moments in life did you feel the happiest and proudest?
- Analyze: what do those moments have in common?
- Measure: how can you measure ongoing success?

All of these go toward understanding what I call our fitness personality. And, as it turns out, your fitness self might not be anything like your work self or family self! When I'm working, I detest distractions. I don't care for small talk. I just want to get to the point, get the work done, and move on. When I'm with friends, I want to laugh and experience things together for lasting memories, lounging over hot tea and feeling unrushed.

Meanwhile, my fitness self probably falls somewhere in the middle of those two. My fitness self won't resonate with some people, but it works for me. To help you better understand this concept and figure out what's most important to you, here's a little rundown on my Fitness Zodiac: The Pira.*

I DON'T NEED VARIETY.

Variety might be the spice of life, but if I had it my way, I'd run 8 to 9 miles every day and be done. I'd not spend a second thinking about abs or stretching or weights, and CrossFit sure as heck wouldn't be on the plan. I'd simply get into my flow, soak up some vitamin D, and enjoy. If that sounds dreadful to you, that's okay; this is my personality! Get your own.

I'M A SOCIAL LONER.

Sorry, what? I really love to run alone. But I also appreciate one or two running buddies for an easy run during the week. I think this is most pronounced when I'm already doing multiple weekly runs over 8 miles in the buildup to a marathon. That gives me plenty of mental time to think and frees me up to chat away on those easy days.

PLANS AND I RARELY WORK.

Without realizing it, from the very beginning, I've listened to my body when it comes to my workouts. I push hard on days I feel good, and go easy when things hurt or I'm sore. This allows me to work out on most days of the week while remaining injury-free. Every time I tried to follow a strict plan, I felt burned out, my love of running dropped, and guess what? There went my built-in motivation!

I never lack the motivation to work out. Which I believe comes full circle to having a lasting why and choosing a sport that fulfills me beyond the calorie burn and far beyond the clock.

Consider how often you have to force yourself to do things like vacuum, scrub the toilets, or eat carrots, while everyone else is having donuts. If your workout is on the same level, then of course, you're going to struggle with motivation!

---

* Related to the standard zodiac signs by virtue of being a Greek word for the element of fire.

"Research suggests that people who engage in personality-appropriate activities will stick with the activities longer, enjoy their workout more and ultimately have a greater overall fitness experience," says Susan Davis-Ali, who created a find-your-fitness-interest profile (no longer available) for Lifetime Fitness, using her PhD in social psychology and years as part of the test publishing industry.

I like it when smart people back up things that I've decided are true. If you're struggling with your why or feeling unmotivated by your workouts lately, then let's discover your fitness personality. Unlike a *Cosmo* quiz, there are no A, B, C answers, and at the end, I won't be telling you which color of running shorts will make you look faster.

I reserve that for the athletes that I coach and then I very much tell them what to do, including to stop adding miles to the plan or to take a freaking rest day.

The Fitness Personality Unquiz Quiz

- Are you more likely to show up if you're accountable to someone? *Try a running group or pick a consistent workout class.*
- At what time of day do you feel your best? *You might not always be able to work out at that time, but try if it will increase enjoyment.*
- Do you thrive on routine? *You gotta be a runner.*
- Do you need variety? *Join an outdoorsy Meet-up group to go kayak, climb, hike, run, bike or join ClassPass for more variety in your cross-training.*
- Do you need intensity or competition to feel accomplished? *Try group workouts, November Project, track clubs.*
- What do you want from a workout? Calm, accomplishment, fun, friendship?
- If you had a motto, would it be no pain no gain? Enjoy the moment? Second place is the first loser?
- What makes you feel the best when you finish a workout?

Did you answer these or skim over them as most of us do when reading a book? Go back, think it through, I'll wait . . . well, actually, I'll go run and you can get back to me. It's worth the three minutes it will take to consider your answers to have more fun with your sweat sessions.

FALL IN LOVE WITH TRAINING

Running doesn't need to be so serious—brows drawn together until you resemble Frida Kahlo and fists clenched, ready to rumble, though I hope not with another runner, just metaphorically with yourself.

It's wasted energy, time, and miles. Although the big banner moment of being handed a hunk of metal to forever hang in your closet may have gotten you started, falling deep in love or at least serious like with training will keep you running long after the finish line.

Those who have flipped that mental switch see each finish merely as a new beginning. Poetic maybe, but mostly a knowing that we thrive in the miles regardless of a race or pace. It's hard to explain to nonrunners why we chose something that takes our toenails, asks us to rise at five a.m. on a Saturday, and often leaves us dreaming of food. But I suppose that's like having kids; you don't get it 'til you're there, so I'm told.

Great, so our new goal is to fall in love with the training. How do we get there?

I'd really, really like to say one step at a time right now, but that's too cliché even for me. Right?

ACT LIKE THE ATHLETE YOU ARE

We've already decided that you're a real runner, so the next step is to begin accepting the title of athlete. Once you pull it on like a varsity letter jacket, you'll start to act accordingly. And not just with a little more swagger in your step.

Maybe you don't forsake all fried foods and anything processed during the race season, like LeBron James, but you do start paying attention to refueling after a run to maximize your recovery because you want to enjoy tomorrow's run, too. You slide down off the deep cushions of your couch each evening to spend some time rolling around the floor in movements that are described with words like *pigeon pose* and *frog pose* and mostly a hilarious invitation to your dog to lick your face.

You are an athlete, choose to act like one.

Spend More Time Happy Dancing

You've got a race on the calendar and that's your focus. Every run is about getting to race day, which is motivating, but not a ton of fun after the first month of training. One bad run makes you question a goal that's months away. Instead, it's time to celebrate the entire process of training.

After knee surgery, I could have been a mess trying to force my recovery or comparing every run to where I used to be. Instead, I decided to go back to what it was like when I first started running and had no expectations of what I could do. Not back to when I used to fake knee pain to get out of running, an irony that is not lost on me, but shortly after that.

I made note of each time that I went slightly farther or picked up the pace the slightest little bit. I quite literally did a Rocky Balboa triumph dance when I completed my first mile running pain-free again. I told my husband daily, to his boredom, how much farther I could extend or bend my leg. You might have thought I was newly discovering what a body could do and it was beautiful. Instead of feeling angst, I was in love with the process of recovery.

What can you start celebrating? Maybe it's a new level of consistency, maybe it's that you smiled more on today's run, maybe it's that you tried a running group, maybe it's that you went literally one single step farther than last week.

Don't wait for the glamorous moments; those are few and far between. Start happy dancing from your actions and progress right now; it tends to beget more progress.

Embrace the Hard

We didn't choose running because it was easy, so you might as well embrace the hard. Knowing that this is a hard you're choosing, provides an immense amount of power. Our instinct is to shy away from hard, but in this case it's the hard that makes it so rewarding.

Although we have things in our lives daily that are difficult, from a boss who always wants more to juggling our time, this is different. It's a place where you can see the results of your work immediately. Each run is an opportunity to challenge your pace, your distance, your mind, and the rewards of that spill over to the rest of your life.

Once you cross the finish line of a distance that once seemed unattainable, the sense that you can tackle anything becomes very real. You remember day one, where running a mile left you winded and tomato faced, yet by showing up consistently, you've accomplished something so much larger. I'm always amazed at how many runners go on to achieve massive things outside running because of the lessons they learned from putting one foot in front of the other repeatedly.

LOVE THE RUN YOU'VE GOT: GOOD AND BAD

On the topic of embracing the hard, I want to throw a really shocking idea out to you. Bad runs are actually pretty great. It sounds ridiculous, but I've come to love those craptastic runs (a technical term, mind you).

I'm not a masochist.

And fine, maybe I'm taking it a little too far to say I love bad runs, but they don't bum me out like when I first started running. Now, I work to embrace them because I've learned that a bad run is an excellent teacher.

Unfortunately, bad runs often come toward the end of a training cycle, particularly for the marathon, which immediately sends us into a spiral of fear and doubt about the pending race. Just when we're looking for that last little bit of confidence, our body betrays us with a run that feels like our first day all over again.

First, a gentle reminder that peak week before taper is designed to push you out of your comfort zone and create stress that allows your body to adapt and grow. But for all the bad runs that simply appear like a life-sucking Dementor from Harry Potter, I offer you this instead: they are a valuable part of training.

How to turn your bad runs into your best teachers? Imagine for a moment that the next time you find yourself near tears, ready to throw your water bottle at the next chirpy passing runner, you begin to reframe this run not as a failure, but as the perfect moment to improve.

Here are the steps we're going to use to make that happen:

1. BAD RUNS REQUIRE OUR ATTENTION.

Bad runs are sometimes the only way your body can get your attention: waving the white flag begging you to stop breaking the rules of too much, too fast, or too long. After a great run, we pat ourselves on the back and go along our merry little way, but a bad run often surprises us and causes us to take notice of what's been going on.

- Are we trying to cram too much into our day?
- Are we stressed out from training, life, trying to get the dog to run with us?
- Do we need another recovery day or was our speed work just harder than normal yesterday?
- Are we skipping the hip, glute, core, stretching, etc.?

Stop trying to overrule your body, and instead, pay attention.

Maybe what you need to pay attention to is your fueling. Marathon training often gives us wiggle room in our calories and we start eating things we normally wouldn't, which can absolutely have an impact on how we feel, how much energy we have, and, oh yes, the digestive system that leads to runner's trots or bonking.

- Did you hydrate well leading up to the run?
- Did you stay on top of electrolytes?
- Did you eat the same thing or something new before this run?
- Did you take in enough or too much fuel while running?

Fueling is different for every runner, which is why you need to keep testing and finding out what works for you. Not just while running, but prerun fuel and fuel throughout the week that helps your body recover from the training.

2. BAD RUNS GIVE US NEW STRENGTH.

If every run were bad, I wouldn't have been at this since 2001. As noted, I'm not a masochist and I'm quite good at going out of my way to avoid things that could hurt. But again, it's during the struggle fest that we take the time to work on an aspect of training that doesn't appear on a plan: toughness.

This isn't about ignoring pain; it's about reminding ourselves of all the runs when it started off rough and then, suddenly, we found a groove, the run began to flow, and we never wanted to stop. Or all the training runs that initially scared us on paper, but we nailed them by taking them one repeat at a time.

A great run makes you feel on top of the world, but a bad run shows you that you're capable of more than you know. Clichéd, trite, whatever, it's true.

While training for my fourth marathon, I found myself with an 18-miler on tap and a tropical storm ripping through Miami, leaving ankle-deep water on every street and winds that would have me swimming with the dolphins.

I saddled up to the only treadmill available. The one without a TV, facing a large brick wall, and I started running. By mile 6, my iPod died, which meant I had nothing but time to evaluate all the reasons I should stop, and for all my love of treadmill running as a great tool, this was not a good day.

I didn't stop. I didn't give in to those negative thoughts. I wouldn't want to do it again soon, but afterward I had a whole new sense of pride and again another tool for reminding myself in life that I can probably handle more than I believe. After your next not-so-wonderful run, look for the new strength you've built that has nothing to do with your legs.

Imagine having that little nugget of wisdom in your gel packet on race day. Speaking of which, why don't they print mantras on those things!* "I've done hard things before and survived, I can do this, too." "This, too, shall pass." "Remember the hard runs, when you kept going."

3. BAD RUNS REMIND US TO BE GRATEFUL.

Finishing a no-good, very bad run, can make you feel surprisingly good once you reframe it with pride and achievement. But, additionally, it gives you a chance to be grateful for all the other runs that you take for granted!

Instead of thinking about the pace you didn't quite nail in a track workout, you're reminded to be grateful that you had the energy to show up, the friends to help push you, and a body that agreed to move pain-free through those repeats.

It reminds you to truly appreciate the runs that make you feel on top of the world and the runs that allow you to explore new places and the runs that allow your best friend to unburden herself a little more easily.

My favorite tool of all time for this is the gratitude mile that I detail in Chapter 9. But when it comes to bad runs, take the time after one to first go through the lessons and then to put that single run into perspective. It was one run, or perhaps a month of runs, among many years of running and find that feeling inside that reminds you how wonderful it is that we *get* to run on any given day.

4. BAD RUNS PLACE THE UNCONTROLLABLES
AND CONTROLLABLES IN ALIGNMENT.

Bad runs are a chance to practice handling all the uncontrollables that could come our way on race day. Not because we'll suddenly find a magic

---

* Note to self: Copyright this idea immediately; you've stumbled upon the next *Shark Tank* idea. Of course, you'll need to find an alternative to gels, since those give you a wonky stomach and no mantra is going to make up for all those extra Porta Potty stops.

wand to control them, but instead, because in our mind we'll now know we can handle them.

Unexpected 99 percent humidity, a random heel blister, bizarre chafing under your right armpit; those moments where you push through these things in training are what you'll remember when you hit the wall on race day. In every race, for every runner, there is a moment of doubt. It might be a split second or miles that drag on, but when it shows up, all the bad runs that you fought through will spring to mind and push you forward. Those frustratingly slow runs will become an energy boost when you truly need it most.

On the flipside, a long, hard slog is also the perfect time to review the controllables. Go back to point one and literally make some notes about what you've been doing recently, to see what could have led to a run that made you want to crawl back under the covers. Don't just file this under "It wasn't my day"; take control of the results you want to achieve.

Did you have a few too many drinks with friends last night? Maybe yogurt before your run? Tried to do your 18 miles a day early, but didn't switch your speed work to another day?

"Get over it—If you have a bad workout or run a bad race, allow yourself exactly 1 hour to stew about it—then move on." Steve Scott, coach and US record holder in the mile, couldn't have said it any better.

The next time you have a particularly horrific run, I invite you to wallow in it, get mad, yell, whatever you need to do. Then, remember that you *get* to run and that run has just taken you one step closer to your goals. Love the run you've got.

EXAMPLES OF NON-PR RUNNING GOALS

If I'm going to tell you that our lives no longer revolve around the clock, I might as well give you some concrete examples. This ensures that when we meet up to run, you don't tell me you couldn't think of anything else to keep you excited.

BE THE BEST RUN FRIEND

Besides my first marathon, the most fun I've ever had on race day was pacing a friend to the finish line of her first marathon; being in Honolulu didn't hurt. You get to embrace the energy, the fanfare, and the coordination of race day without the pressure of running your own personal best. Maybe you have a friend nervous about her first 5K or 10; volunteer to run beside her as a cheerleader and support system.

Helping someone else is its own boost, but also reminds you how much you've learned about running when you become a teacher of sorts. You have knowledge that's valuable, which reinforces your own belief that you're a runner!

On race day, your friend might be more relaxed with your help navigating the start area and then simply having you beside them to point out water stops or ask if he or she is okay. Finding out how your friend needs to be motivated is a process, so remember that not everyone will want to chat the whole time or have you yelling *"We are the champions, no time for losers, come on, let's go!"* for 26 miles.

CHALLENGE YOURSELF WITH A NEW DISTANCE/RACE STYLE

It's an automatic PR if you run a new distance, which means you can simply enjoy the first go around knowing that you'll be able to improve next time.

Instead of worrying about your time, use it as a learning experience. What's different when you go longer or shorter? What will you need to do differently next time? Did you enjoy it more or realize that you needed to change your training to try it again?

A few easy ways to switch it up, even if you've been running a long time:

- A 10-mile race (these are becoming much easier to find)
- A Spartan race

- A trail race
- A night race
- A team relay during a marathon
- A 200-mile team relay
- A race at altitude
- A net downhill race

Even running your tenth half marathon doesn't mean it's the same or should be compared to your last race. A half marathon that drops 2,000 feet is a whole different experience from a rolling trail half marathon. Remembering that can also take the focus off the clock and put it back on doing your best with the current conditions.

BRING IN THE CHA-CHING INSTEAD OF BLING

Want more kids drinking clean water in Africa? Want more kids eating three meals a day in the United States? Want a bib to some of the hardest-to-get-into marathons in the world?

Partnering with a charity can be a bit self-serving if it means doing it to get a race bib, but who cares?! You're doing something fantastic for the world and for yourself at the same time; I see no harm in that. Besides, it's nearly impossible not to think about those your funds will help while training.

You'll see many runners on race day with a photo or a name on their shirt to honor loved ones they raised money to support or in their memory. Knowing that the race is for someone else adds a new dimension to training and a determination to show up no matter how hard it gets.

First, you're focused on someone else's pain, which helps keep your annoyingly bad runs in perspective. Second, you're forced to interact with people to collect donations or train together. Even though we runners often appreciate our alone time, the health benefits of connecting with others is massive, just check out *Blue Zones*, by Dan Buettner. Based on his studies of the healthiest aging populations around the world, not only was activity a commonality, but so was community and connection.*

Third, you're no longer doing this just for you, which takes away some of the guilt people feel for the time needed to train. I admit that one is hard for me because I know I'm a better human to be around after a run, so guilt need not apply.

If you're not interested in a big race, but know that helping others will motivate you, then check out any of the great apps, such as Charity Miles, which donate based on the miles you run during training. No walking around the office asking for donations; it happens simply because you train.

Snag a Running Partner

As a mostly solo runner, like many of you, I choose running time to disconnect and think. But there's simply too much research proclaiming the benefits of running with others to ignore it. Get over your fear of joining a running group, put forth a little extra effort to meet up with a friend one day each week, or start making your get-togethers more fitness focused.

I won't know anyone.

I'll be the slowest person there.

They might be zombies.

Yes, you will be the new kid on the block and maybe you will be the slowest.** I've now run with groups in cities across the United States and work through these thoughts every time because the result is worth the discomfort (*hmmm, does that sound like a runner mind-set or what?*)!

---

* Not just any community, but being involved with healthier or happier people ensured that they, too, enjoyed those qualities. Community is a big part of what keeps so many runners going. It's a sense of belonging with others who get you. If you can't find it in person, jump online and you'll find tons of forums, social media, and other ways to connect.

** On the off chance you meet people at a run group who are negative about your chosen pace, just know the papers will refer to them as a jogger someday and they probably don't nod, either.

To be clear, a group doesn't need to be thirty people or include runners you don't like; you can find a friend or two that you enjoy running with . . . you just often find them by first attending that big group.

The reality is that runners don't care. **Runners *love* meeting other runners,** anyone who will allow us to talk about our chosen passion and relish all the little details that make our dear nonrunning friends' eyes glaze over.

A few more reasons to psych yourself up to test out group running:

- Accountability to show up for workouts
- Someone else to celebrate your achievements
- Structured workouts
- Access to experienced runners with tons of knowledge
- Reasons to run that don't involve calories
- Ability to help other new runners stick with it
- Getting out despite the weather and then relishing it later as you retell the stories
- Encouragement to hit key paces in speed work
- Someone to race with, which can be great for pacing
- Great friends = great fun for running and life
- People who will gladly talk about all aspects of running
- Discounts on gear and events
- Safety for all those dark early mornings

And if you decide to go the charity route for a race, you'll find that often comes with a built-in training group. Win-win.

ALTERNATIVE WORKOUT GOALS

I'm about to commit a cardinal sin of the passionate runner and suggest that you might find goals that are not 100 percent running related. Calm down, Karen, I'm not saying you need to stop running.

Lifting weights is not my cup of tea, but while injured, I was determined to continue moving my body and choosing exercises that would eventually make me a better runner when I rehabbed. Luckily, that led me to try a variety of things from TRX to spin class to the Pilates Reformer.

All of them benefit our running in different ways, but setting a non-PR goal of becoming a more well-rounded, injury-proof athlete is pretty spectacular. Once you're back to marathon training, you'll find it much easier to continue making these things part of your routine because you started experiencing the same thrill of progress as you did with running. Additionally, the time away usually makes you appreciate running even more. That's right; even if I don't always enjoy the deep stretch of pigeon pose, I do enjoy knowing I get to run tomorrow feeling strong and pain-free.

You Can't Phone In Consistency

What happens when your body no longer allows you to run the way you used to? I know this all too well, as do many runners who go through an injury, illness, or simply age. Instead of focusing on the pace, start going back to basics and focus on showing up consistently.

Not only is there motivation in seeing yourself show up in the hard times, but consistency creates habits. Habits mean you don't need to think about whether you'll go on a long run today; you simply do because that's what happens every Sunday.

Consistency might be one of my favorite words, so it's no surprise I think this is a stellar goal for any runner. And it's usually what I point to when people ask how I maintain motivation year after year.

Maybe you've got it figured out with the miles, but need to be consistent with hip mobility, postrun stretching, postrun nutrition, a dynamic warmup, or cross-training.

Pick a single area and focus on it for the next three months. Becoming consistent in any one of those will play a role in improving your runs; when your runs feel better, you want to do more; and doing more usually leads to great new race results.

DIVERSIFY YOUR ROUTE

With your eyes closed, you can map out the route from your door through the neighborhood, past the barking dog behind an iffy fence, the random discarded sneaker, and back home to equal 3 miles. Repetition is comforting because we can zone out, but it can also lead to boredom by knowing exactly what to expect.

Set a goal to mix it up once a week with a trail, a new path, a group run; create funny patterns on your Strava map; try to hit every road near you. Switching up your route will also help prevent such issues as IT (iliotibial) band syndrome, which can occur from running on the same side of the road over and over again, where it's slightly slanted for water runoff.

Don't feel like hopping in the car to drive to a new location? Don't. Play a mental game of choosing to go left where you would normally go right. Immediately, you've reengaged your senses and the feel of the run is going to change. Instead of zoning out, you're awake, aware, and engaged.

Maybe now is the time to test out trail running by driving somewhere on Saturdays when you have extra time. Trails will challenge you mentally and physically in ways that help you continue growing as a runner. After fifteen years of road running, which I love, I moved to Denver and found myself inundated with invites to hit the trails. I was terrified!

Suddenly, running downhill required a whole new set of sensory skills that I have not yet totally mastered. Running uphill at 5,000 feet with rocks moving gets all those little muscles around your ankles and knees fired up. Although people love to talk about the softer surface being good for our body, I think the change in scenery is the real benefit.

With a fresh view, that long uphill climb isn't just about praying for a good downhill on the other side; it's taking a moment to pause and really look around at the world. It's the quiet that's different from an early-morning neighborhood just waking up and it's the vistas of snow-capped mountains or fields that go on for ages.

Whether you opt for a new paved path or a trail you've tried only a few times, the change will give your running new life. A huge part of the allure of running for many of us is that we can simply step out the front door and go. We don't need a gym, don't waste time trying to get somewhere, and always finish right where we want to be.

However, the more I traveled the world and of course, as we moved around the United States from Kansas City to Miami and finally Denver, I noticed my excitement level each time I laced up in a new place. It's time for adventure, which often leads me to run a great deal farther because I need to see what's around the next corner.

A RUNNING STREAK

A running streak is considered a string of days where you run at least 1 mile every single day. Annual challenges pop up around New Year's, which can be a great way to use community support to boost your motivation.

However, I'm torn on this recommendation because I see both the value and the potential for major issues. Personally, I'm not a fan of streaking for most runners because of injuries, burnout, and the motivation fallout from missing a day.

But a short-term streak might be exactly what you need to get addicted to that sweaty runner's high. It forces you to think more creatively about how to maximize your time and to enjoy running in random new places to make it happen: No time after work? Then, you'll need to figure out packing your briefcase with extra clothes for a runch session. Gotta drop the kids off at practice? Might as well run some laps around the field while they warm up.

One of the biggest excuses for not sticking to a training plan is time; a running streak often shows runners just how much time they have to make it happen or reminds them that a few miles are still better than no miles.

If you decide to make this your goal, remember to listen to your body and, when it starts to cry "uncle," stop. It's most definitely an ego boost to say you've run 120 days straight, but if you're in pain for half of those days or so tired you can't function, is it really useful?

RACE WITH SOMEONE

Going beyond training with a group, have you ever raced with someone? Not that homestretch moment where you battle it out, but working together from step one for a shared goal. It brings a whole new dimension to race day. If, like me, you race infrequently, having a friend alongside can help you first relax and then, as the miles pass, not talk yourself out of a goal.

Maybe now is the perfect time to organize a girls' trip that culminates in a half marathon! Maybe it's time to try being a mentor for an organization like Girls on the Run. Or maybe you consistently race with the same person and might just need to try sharing it with someone else for an entirely new experience.

This shifts the focus from what's happening on your watch to the people around you, reminding you to laugh, giggle even, and enjoy the journey.

CONFESSIONS OF A RUN COACH

I know you want to believe we coaches are perfect; we want to believe it, too. In case you've been having a case of the Shoulds lately, here are a few things that are reportedly good for us, that I don't do.

#1 Kale Chips—Too expensive to buy and too lazy to make, this fantastic snack rarely passes my lips.

#2 10 oz Water per Mile While Running—I can't stand the slosh, so I'd rather be a bit dehydrated.

#3 No Eating After 7 p.m.—This is a Bob Harper rule designed to keep you from snacking on less-than-stellar foods. Sometimes, I haven't eaten enough at that point and I'm hungry, so I eat.

#4 No Eating in Front of the TV—I know how important it is to be mindful, but there's something very relaxing for me about taking a break from thinking about what to write next by getting lost in someone else's story while I enjoy my power bowl. If I could easily read and eat, I'd do that instead.

#5 Get a Trainer—I hate being told what to do in general. I really don't like it when you're pushing me out of my comfort zone. I prefer to do that on my own terms.

#6 Lift Really Heavy Things—I did start increasing the weights I'm lifting, but I have zero desire ever to do Olympic lifts like my CrossFitting friends. "Good for you, not for me," in the words of Amy Poehler.

#7 Cold Shower Therapy—Tons of great research on a cold morning shower getting you started with focus and fat burning . . . nope, still not gonna do it.

CHAPTER 3

BREAKING DOWN DISCOMFORT VS. PAIN

With every footfall, the pain was getting sharper, the needles more piercing, the throbbing more like a bass drum, and the shrieks in my mind began to escape through my mouth.

"I can't freaking do this!"

This elicited chuckles and pitying glances from racers nearby who understood the mental war of the marathon miles, but didn't know I was ensconced in a battle that went far beyond overcoming the dreaded wall. And then one voice, I'd say an angel's but the head-to-toe neon makes that questionable, *"Hey, we're not trying to win this thing; let's walk together for a bit and then try running again."*

Walk?! Who let this woman out of the psych ward for a race? Real runners don't walk; everyone knows that. Turns out that only a novice, ego-driven, clock-watching runner believes that. I'd like to blame it on my youth, but it was probably also fueled by having started a blog where I then shared my big, hairy goals and feeling that I would let others down by acquiescing to the pain.

The San Diego marathon became a turning point for me in two key ways:

1. I learned that there is an enormous difference between discomfort and pain.
2. I learned that there is joy in the process, not just the finish line.

I lied; the third thing I learned is that badass runners walk. Some of them use the run-walk method to achieve Boston Qualifying times; some of them use a full seven hours on their feet to walk a marathon, which is incredibly freaking hard; some of them simply know when walking will serve them better than the peg-legged shuffle I was doing.

It was 2007; I had a whopping 1 marathon under my belt and about five years of consistent running. My friends were all pushing for Boston Qualifying times, thus I adopted this as my goal, too, even though in my heart of hearts, it really didn't matter that much to me. I still just thought running was a pretty freaking amazing thing that I'd convinced my body to do.

Like any great runner who knows it all, I had a well-crafted training plan from five minutes of Googling. I found the pace I would need to run and set about running that pace for every single run. Yes, all of them. All the time. Constantly.

I can actually feel you shaking your head right now, which simply means you're smarter than I was at age twenty-five; congratulations. But stop it; that makes it very hard to keep reading.

The net result was that ten weeks into training, I began experiencing sharp pains on the outside of my knee, which began to travel like a freight train up my leg to my hip. I studiously ignored them and continued to train, because running hurts, right? If I paid attention to every niggle, naggle, and itch* I'd never make it farther than the first few steps of a run.

---

* *Niggle* is a word I so often use that I'm shocked to find most people have no idea what I'm saying. Maybe it's a midwestern thing? Anyhow, a niggle is a slight, but persistent

During a 16-mile out-and-back training run leading up to San Diego, I found myself at mile 8 unable to walk, let alone run without searing pain.

Again, being the genius that I am, I refused to carry a cell phone (back in the flip phone days) and was forced to walk, sit, crawl, and sob my way home.* At which point, I relented to seek help. I found a sports medicine doctor who taught me about this very common injury called iliotibial band syndrome (a.k.a. fiery pain shooting up your leg, followed by the feeling of being stabbed in the knee).

He said it was caused by increasing mileage, pace, or intensity too quickly. Guilty on all three, I cried about the upcoming race and then he gave me a cortisone shot. Within a few hours, I could see why athletes found this shot magical; the pain was vanishing. Years later, I learned it's a great tool for muscle rehabilitation, but a much trickier topic when it comes to your joints. So, this is not a promotion to head out and start asking for shots.

In the remaining weeks, I backed off intense training and lined up at that marathon with the goal of pushing hard, but no Boston Qualifying attempt. Everything seemed to be clicking until mile 13, when that IT band once again let me know I'd done too much. But with the real-runners-must-dig-deep mind-set, I didn't stop.

I walked the remaining 13 miles, at some points taking twenty-five minutes to complete a mile. And once again without a phone, I borrowed one from a spectator to give my husband a heads-up on my delay. I could have more wisely pulled out of the race, but that wasn't an option I fully understood had value, yet.

Real runners dig deep and push through; that's what made them so incredible in my eyes. Except that's completely bananas, whack, whatever hip term I don't know. Elite runners pull out of races if something is

---

annoyance. Meanwhile, *naggle*, I assumed, was a made-up word to fit the sentence, but appears to mean "to dispute pettily."

* Let's be honest; I could have found a pay phone, begged to use someone's phone, or any multitude of things. But I was deep in the "I'm a freaking runner, I can't stop" mind-set.

wrong because one race is not worth the potential long-term recovery or injury. Even smart middle-of-the-packers recognize that there's a point where you've crossed the line from normal "this is really freaking hard" to "my body is telling me something is seriously wrong."

As a result of my particular stupidity, I couldn't run for six months after that race. I couldn't walk for almost two weeks without crying. And I'm quite sure I made everyone around me miserable as well. Although finishing that race was absolutely not worth it, the entire experience allowed me to become a much different runner and a coach who helps people head off these major injuries through smarter training.

I fell in love with running in a whole new way: no longer feeling the need to chase the same goals as my peers, but instead finding the goals that lit me up and drove me to continue through hard Kansas City winters and hot, humid Miami summers.

I became the runner who since that day has been a vigilant member of the Must Warm Up Before Every Single, Solitary Mile Club. And a founding member of the Never Forget That Prehab Is Better Than Rehab Team! The names are a little long, but dues are currently being waived and membership is open for both, if you're interested.

Combining those, I created a system that allowed me to put my IT band issues behind me for the last decade and to avoid any other major injuries because of my running. I would be remiss not to note that I did, as mentioned, have knee surgery in 2017. Although some of the worn cartilage could potentially be attributed to running with my kneecap not properly aligned, my orthopedic surgeon immediately agreed that running was not the root of my issues. The overnight inability to straighten my leg was likely the result of the previous day's entertainment at the trampoline park.

But this isn't a book about me (mostly), it's a book designed to help you be a smarter runner than I was back then. Learn from my stupidity that though running may often feel hard, it need not be truly painful. Injuries are not a foregone conclusion and pain is not inevitable; these are myths we need to break free of. Equally important is that they're no more the mark of a runner than a specific race time.

WHY WE RUN THROUGH PAIN

Running is inherently uncomfortable. Not to put a damper on our fun, but it's true. If running were easy, we'd call it taking a stroll in the park, which is a downright perfect way to spend a sunny afternoon with a good friend.

Is it possible we've simply come to enjoy that pain? Yikes.

Want to get faster? Push yourself just outside your comfort zone, where it hurts a little.

Want to go farther? Keep putting one foot after the other even though every muscle is screaming to quit.

Want to hit a new personal best? Fight through the searing lungs and burning legs 'til you see the finish line.

Pain registers differently when you've become accustomed to mind over matter. This is absolutely a key factor in progressing as runners and one of our many superpowers. Which is why once we start to notice an issue, we first push it aside, then convince ourselves on a completely irrational level that perhaps this run won't hurt. Maybe if we just slow it down a bit; nope. Okay, maybe if we try picking up the pace a bit; nope. Okay, what if I start running backward for a while?

In some ways, it's fantastic that we've gotten our brain to this point through training. It means that we can move through those niggles and, after an injury, avoid a spiral of fear. But of course, there's the massive issue of when we use those tools to ignore actual injuries.

If we're being completely honest with ourselves, there's an awful lot of chatter among runners about what currently hurts. A little ache on the top of our foot elicits plenty of ideas for relacing our shoes, and issues with side stitches turn into a conversation about how dairy leads Anna to break out horribly along her nose but also makes it hard for her to breathe on the run.

At times, we wear our aches and pains like a badge of honor. Which is part of the problem. Running isn't supposed to hurt. It's going to be hard and uncomfortable as our body adapts, but it really isn't meant to hurt. Which, of course, is why our nonrunning counterparts don't understand these conversations or why we won't just take some days off when in pain.

What is it that drives us to continue attempting the miles despite pain and perhaps feeling even more driven because of the pain? One of the key reasons so many of us are driven to run is the way it makes us feel. Running isn't just a workout, and it isn't just about the endorphin rush.

- Running usually gets us outdoors, which is a refreshing change from the rest of the day.
- Running is a time to think, mull, ponder.
- Running is also a time to finally stop thinking, mulling, and pondering.
- Running is alone time.
- Running is connecting-with-friends time.
- Running allows us to challenge ourselves and to define the limitations of that challenge.
- Running gives us a daily accomplishment.
- Running ties us to a larger community.

Darn it, it just feels good to move.

Or maybe we push through because we have a goal-driven personality? We don't know how to stop before the goal is achieved. It's often said that most runners are a bit type A: driven, focused, always looking for that little edge to improve. And once we've committed ourselves to a new distance or a new pace, it's nearly impossible for us to quit until the finish line is crossed.

It's why the finish-line medical tent is littered with people who would normally be considered extremely healthy. But when our logical mind is screaming that the pain is too great and we need to stop and recover, our emotional brain is screaming, *"Charrrrrrge, take no prisoners!"* Something about that finish line feels as if we've mastered the universe. We might not get the promotion, decorate the perfect Pinterest party cookies, or show up on time for PTA, but gawd bless it, we *can* do this. It feels good to get the win, even if we realize there's a price to pay.

In fact, there's a lot of fear that plays into our need to run despite the pain. What if we gain back the weight we lost? What if we lose our friendship circle because we can't go on Saturday long runs? What if we can't ever get back to where we were after the time off?

All these emotions lead us to override our logical thoughts and, instead of resting, to continue pushing our limits, resulting in form that breaks down, forcing weak muscles to try even harder to compensate, and straining because we've overreached. These are the moments when we often go from a niggle to a full-blown out-for-the-season injury. Which means our job is not only the prehab that is defined in Chapter 4, but the mental work of trusting our body.

Know that pulling back for a day or week is the smarter way to achieve our big goals, through consistent training, rather than putting on blinders and pushing through for a short-term win. It's walking a constant fine line to not lose the drive to embrace discomfort for growth, but also learn to be kind to ourselves when the body is asking us to stop, drop, and roll.*

THE DIFFERENCE BETWEEN DISCOMFORT AND PAIN

As a beginning runner, each new distance means muscle soreness and stretching our mental fortitude.

---

* Honestly, I'm just really proud of that analogy after talking about my IT band being on fire and wanted to point it out. But also, you'll see in the section ahead that if things feel as if they are on fire, that's a really great sign you're injured.

As an experienced runner, each new goal means pushing the body to handle more stress.

Too much stress and the body topples like pulling out that last wobbly piece in a Jenga puzzle. Which brings us back to the original question: in seeking discomfort to improve, how do we recognize when a line has been crossed and we're on the precipice of injury?

Aches and pains are how the body tells you something isn't right. If you're training appropriately, meaning no leaps from a single ten-minute mile to 7 miles at an eight-minute pace in a month, and you've learned to work on your form and include some basic strength work, this shouldn't happen. You don't have to live with pain. Let me reiterate this startling revelation: running is not supposed to hurt.

How can you tell whether that feeling in your calf is discomfort and the body growing stronger or the beginning of an injury? By paying attention, rather than ignoring it.

RED FLAGS

Let's start with the most obvious signs that you have an injury and it's not your brain playing tricks on you for asking it to do hard things:

- Swelling
- An area that is painful to the touch
- Numbness
- Difficulty moving
- Radiating pain

Additionally, anything that alters your running form is an immediate red flag. For example, your big toe has started to hurt, so to ignore it, you've begun rolling your foot slightly outward. Suddenly you've changed the pressure on your knee and the twist of your hips, and what might have been a strained tendon in your foot turns into knee pain.*

---

* I know these seem obvious, but if runners actually paid attention to these signals, this whole chapter would be unnecessary. We're like toddlers who've been told not to stick

Finally, if you're popping anti-inflammatories before every run "just in case" or because you can't make it through without them, do I really need to tell you this is an issue? By now, I'm sure you've seen the science stating that all those pills prior to a run are beating the heck out of your liver. And I'm sure you're absolutely aware that continuing to run on something so painful is probably not helping it get better. Kind of like pushing on a bruise in an attempt to heal it.

Don't be a hero; just stop. Don't Google it; you'll always find out they're going to amputate. Don't tell yourself it's just one more run, because there's always another one after that.

Log on to your health-care website and find a sports medicine doctor; these tend to be the best at getting to the root of the problem and understand that runners are not great with simply being told to rest. In fact, if you find yourself at a doctor whose sole advice is to rest, then you have my permission to run out the door and to another doctor. Rest alone is not the cure. But more on that in Chapter 4, where I extoll my love of physical therapy.

Sports doctors aren't reserved for NFL players; they're available to us middle-of-the-packers. Don't be afraid to utilize them. Not sure which doctor you need to see? Here's a short breakdown of options:

- Urgent Care: If you think it's broken or it's bleeding, just do it. Usually these stand-alone facilities are cheaper than going to an emergency room, but they may not always have all the necessary equipment. Call ahead to check if you're wondering about an x-ray. During a lovely Colorado stroll with my mom, she fell off the sidewalk (yes, off, all by herself; I did not push her and I stand by that claim), and heading to urgent care was faster and cheaper to get her quick attention and the diagnosis of a broken foot.
- Orthopedic Specialist: If you're having severe pain in your knee joint, foot, or hips, this could be a good option because it's often

---

something in the light socket, but need an adult to put on a plastic cover anyway because we just keep trying.

caused by repetitive motion or a specific trauma. Orthopedists deal with bones, joints, and nerves, which means they're equipped to diagnose and provide treatment recommendations. Again, if you have the opportunity to find someone who works with athletes, that's ideal, and don't feel tied to the first recommendation you receive. I spoke to three different doctors before deciding what type of surgery to have on my knee.

- Podiatrist: If you're having pain in your foot specifically, this is the doctor for you. It could be a stress fracture or plantar fasciitis—both are common in runners, and can be resolved with treatment.

- Chiropractor: If you're in the red flag zone, this may not be the solution you need, but it's one that has worked for me and athletes I coach regularly. Hip pain, knee pain, and back pain can all be the result of the body's being out of alignment. Running when your hips aren't level means that with every single foot strike, muscles are trying to compensate and overcorrect. A once-a-month adjustment was key to resolving my IT band issues when they first began. And it bears repeating: I really like finding someone with a sports focus because that person will also work on tight muscles, not just cracking your back.

- Physical Therapist (PT): I reserve this option for longtime runners or those who are in tune with their body, to start here before seeing a doctor. For example, a year after knee surgery, I went back to the PT once every few months as I noticed little issues cropping up. In those sessions, we identified potential muscle weaknesses or any changes to my form and created a series of exercises to continue building strength.

You'll notice I did not list your primary care physician. If you're required to get a referral for insurance purposes, then absolutely go to a PCP. Otherwise, the majority of athletes I've worked with walk away from those visits frustrated by the simple statement they should rest or run less. That's advice we rarely follow and doesn't resolve the underlying issue.

GET CONNECTED (SANS TECHNOLOGY)

While I hope you try to disconnect from your calendar, text messages, and phone calls when you lace up, it's largely to ensure that you finally reconnect with your body. Sans the multitude of distractions, you start getting a feel for how hard you breathe at different paces and whether you start throwing on the brakes or opening up your stride to cruise downhill. During any run, take a few moments to scan your body and tune into the sensations. If something is beginning to hurt with every stride or showing up on every run, it's time to take action.

Longtime runners become so in tune with their body, they instinctively know when something isn't right. It helps them head off colds, injuries, and drive crazy doctors who keep saying they seem so healthy, but usually they're right and an issue needs to be addressed.

SWITCH TABS MENTALLY

Multitasking has become the new sitting disease apparently, but in this case, it's going to work to your benefit. We all know that playing mind games during the run helps us go just a bit farther or ignore that dirty little Margie.

When it comes to pain, test out the issue by metaphorically opening a new tab in your brain. If you divert your attention to another line of thinking, such as what's for lunch (I always hope the answer is pizza) or doing a hard math problem, does that pain suddenly stop interrupting your thoughts? If so, it's likely more mental than a true injury.

Your brain wants to protect you from pushing too far, which is why it throws up these roadblocks. Our job is to listen to the ones with big blinking red lights and then pay attention to, but not freak out over, the orange caution cones. Except on race day; then, be really aware of those cones because I have tripped over them trying to get out of being bunched in a pace group, and that hurts.

PAIN TOLERANCE SCALE

One of the fantastic things about running is that it increases our pain tolerance threshold. Once you've made yourself run for two hours at six a.m.

on a 26-degree morning while the family is at home flipping pancakes, stubbing your toe is just a minor annoyance.

The downside is that we runners often don't seek help or address an issue until it's become intolerable pain, because we've changed our perception of pain. At that point, you've got a big mess on your hands, which means it's going to take longer to correct and recover from. Instead, when you start to notice something cropping up, try rating it on your own personal pain scale of 1 to 10. Then, take note:

- Is it staying the same?
- Getting worse?
- Worse with specific movements?

A dull ache can often be overridden with changing our thoughts; sharp, shooting pains that force you to stop are a sign that something larger is happening. Consider sharp pain your signal to immediately stop. Do not pass Go. Do not collect $200. Do not try to "tough it out" or rub dirt on it—I don't know why that's recommended for an injury, but still don't do it.

All these will help you learn when to let it go and when to take action.

TIGHTNESS THAT DISSIPATES

If your stride feels off or uncomfortable in the first few miles, but fades the longer you run, it may simply be a signal to extend your warm-up and include some dynamic stretches to activate muscles.

When we first hop out of bed, our muscles are stiff and cold from a night of sleeping. Without taking the time to increase blood flow, increase mobility, and prime our body for activity, it's extremely easy to create an injury. Tightness at the beginning of a workout is a sign that your body isn't ready and will inhibit proper running form, plus it's just not enjoyable.

If you experience the opposite, which is a run that's going well initially, but then you begin to feel your calves cramping up or your hamstrings feeling tighter and tighter, it's time to do some investigation. Are you low on electrolytes, are you running on the balls of your feet, are you altering your stride to compensate for the tightness? Usually this is a precursor to an injury, so don't ignore it!*

PAIN YOU CAN PINPOINT

If the location of your pain is at a joint and occurs repeatedly, it's time to get things checked out by a professional and stop wondering what's wrong. Occasionally (taper week specifically), you'll have a random ache that never appears again; I call this race week phantom pains, which occur as your body adjusts to the change in training and prepares to peak on race day.

However, most of the time, pain that is directly in or around a joint should be addressed. Although the joint might be the spot expressing the pain, it could be caused by surrounding tight muscles. Don't let it freak you out; instead, find a sports medicine doctor who'll look at your movement patterns, check muscles, and often take an x-ray just to eliminate any major concerns.

More often than not, you'll be sent on your way with a prescription for physical therapy. These extremely smart persons will ask how often you stretch, work your hip strength, and activate your glutes. Hopefully after reading this book, you'll be able to proudly say, "I do prehab before every run!" If that's not the case, may the force be with you and why did you even buy this?

COMMON RUNNING PAINS

Feel that you're still not sure what's what? Here's an additional breakdown to help with some of the most common issues runners face. We'll talk more in Chapter 4 about how to prevent injuries and dealing with

---

* I'm sure it's beginning to feel as if I want you to become Sherlock Holmes, investigating every little thing about your body. That's not entirely wrong, but more accurately, I want you to be willing to pay attention and to find out what's going to work best for you to keep running with less pain.

some of these aches, pains, and twinges, but for now, let's ensure that we know what's a glaring red light and when you've got a yellow to proceed with caution.

First up, we have the age-old reason all nonrunners believe we're destroying our body: knee pain.

- Knee pain caused by tight muscles
- Knee pain caused by poor running form (slamming your heel into the ground)
- Knee pain caused by weak hips (allowing the knee to fall inward)

Let's help prove them all wrong by getting on board the prehab train and only having injuries to things like our ego when we trip over a cracked sidewalk in front of a large group of middle schoolers waiting for the bus. Completely hypothetical situation, along with the hypothetically skinned hands and knees that may or may not have made said runner cry.

KNEE PAIN AFTER RUNNING

A slight ache could be your knees' adjusting to the new level of impact. This isn't entirely bad, as we know it helps to lubricate the joint and as your muscles get stronger this will stop. Try wearing compression gear and slow down the increase in your mileage to allow the body time to adapt.

A sharp pain on the outside of your knee could be from a tight IT band, whereas a deep pain at the front of your knee could be runner's knee. There's a lot at play, from weak hips to tight calves, which is why we so often see pain manifest in our knees though they may not be the actual issue.

PAIN IN YOUR SIDE

More likely than not, you've got a garden-variety side stitch. Why do you get pain in your side when running? Your body is adapting to the new level of breathing needed to run and your diaphragm is contracting. Slow down, take some deep breaths, and stretch. This, too, will get better over time.

Alternatively, you could have enjoyed a large meal and your body is trying to digest your food while sending blood to your legs. Eventually, it gives up on your stomach to keep your legs pumping, and that leads to stomach discomfort.

PAIN IN THE FRONT OF YOUR SHIN

Accurately labeled shin splints, this common issue is almost entirely avoidable. Don't increase your miles too quickly, ensure you're wearing the right shoes, stretch your calf muscles, and don't try to muscle through it. If they've already started to appear, bust out the compression gear, start with ice, then move to heat, and for once I am going to say the dreaded words "rest your overworked muscles."

PAIN IN YOUR FOOT

Every step requires your foot to absorb immense amounts of impact, and it's not uncommon for them to be sore or tired after a long run (especially if your shoes are worn down). But once it becomes a constant ache in your heel that's noticeably worse in the mornings, you've crossed over into an injury known as plantar fasciitis.

Or if you're consistently feeling pressure on the top of your foot, a simple relacing of your shoes could relieve the pressure. But an ongoing ache could be the precursor to a stress fracture, another common runner injury from upping the mileage faster than our body can adapt or from nutritional choices that aren't supporting our new mileage.

PAIN IN YOUR HIP

Sitting all day long causes tight hip flexors, which are then often made tighter if we choose to opt out of embracing the foam roller or spending a little time on stretching. The majority of the time, we can loosen, strengthen, and warm up our muscles enough to eliminate this pain. But if you're feeling it right in the joint or noticing swelling, seek out a professional opinion to get a resolution.

If any of these issues warrant attention, get it now. Waiting not only prolongs your mental misery, but usually the time it takes to recover. And recovery is a both physical and mental process.

HOW TO MENTALLY RECOVER FROM AN INJURY

It's not that runners are bad patients, it's that we have very little patience for sitting around. Invariably, all that time on our hands leads to excessive pity parties, which is not to say I don't love me a good Hallmark movie day of tear-soaked tissues, but that's just part of the journey to get you running again.

While there's abundant information on physical recovery, we also need a plan to mentally and emotionally bounce back. We feel a little out of control without our stress relief and a little crazy when others don't understand our tears over being told to spend a few weeks on the couch. This is your permission slip to have all the emotions you need to have, because it's part of the recovery process. And for anyone who tells you "it's a blessing in disguise," you have permission to kick them in the shin and ask whether that feels like a blessing.

STEP 1: THROW YOURSELF A PITY PARTY.

First things first: it's okay to be sad. You just spent months (maybe even years) preparing for your event, and if you weren't furiously disappointed, I'd be concerned. Of course, you're upset! Angry. Questioning every little thing you might have done differently. Wallow in it—at least for a little while.

Let yourself actually feel your icky, confusing, stuck-in-the-bottom-of-the-hole feelings. You deserve time to grieve for the way your best-laid plans and biggest dreams fell apart. Don't skip this phase; you won't be doing yourself or anyone who later tries to ply you with wonderful clichés any favors.

But you also have to put a time frame on it. You get exactly two days to pity party hardy, then you make a plan.

STEP 2: IGNORE EVERYONE WHO BRIGHTLY SAYS, "IT'LL MAKE YOU A BETTER RUNNER."

Listen, your friends really do have the best of intentions with the world of clichés about to come your way. And yet I really want to print up a shirt that says, "I'm not grateful for this injury."

In the grand scheme of life, we can fully recognize that our injury is a minor thing. We even know that in our own lives, we've faced harder things, such as losing a family member to illness, but at the moment it's allowed to be our big, horrible thing.

Next up, let your friends know that you appreciate their well wishes, but you'd prefer chocolate. Or since you aren't running, maybe you'd prefer green juice. Either way, gifts not platitudes.

STEP 3: START A DAILY GRATITUDE PRACTICE.

On the heels of everything I just said, here's some real talk: *it could be worse*. Once you've thrown yourself the grandest pity party, it's time to get some perspective.

One of the ways I did this was to immediately figure out **what I could still do**.

Can't walk much, but I can bike.

Can't do lunges, but my upper body is fully functional for some killer strength workouts.

Can't run long distances, but trails seem to feel a little better for some hiking or short runs.

Since our standard tool for dealing with stress or working through issues has been removed, it's time to embrace this whole mindfulness thing. There are lots of ways to go about it that don't involve meditation, though that's a pretty great tool:

- Try the Five-Minute Journal to help you stick to a daily gratitude practice.
- Walk and listen to people like Louise Hay and Esther Hicks, who focus on choosing better thoughts.
- Consider adding mindfulness to your day, which simply means being more present and more aware as you do things.
- Take a few big, wonderful deep breaths.
- Sit outside and soak up some nature.*

STEP 4: MAKE REHAB YOUR NEW SPORT.

"I ran twenty miles last weekend and now I can't walk the length of the grocery store!" If I had a dollar for each time I said something like that. Because, yeah, injury is demoralizing, especially when you've got plans that you've announced to the world! Look at me, I'm running this race, aiming for that PR, sponsored by a great company . . . oh and PS, now I can't do diddly.

But what if, instead of moaning about all the fitness you've lost, you make rehab your new sport?

I'm consistent with prehab, but fanatical about *rehab.* Do all those exercises and stretches with the same focus you'd give to a tough interval session on the track. Earn yourself a PR in "most consistent injury recovery."

This type of work will never feel as fun and freeing as a long run, but getting serious about it instead of binge-watching Netflix while you dive face-first into a chocolate cake is what will get you on the road to full recovery. (You should probably have a little of that cake, too, though.)

STEP 5: GIVE YOURSELF PERMISSION
TO LOVE OTHER THINGS.

You had to pull out of your goal race. You went from being in the best shape of your life to . . . not. The season is ruined.

---

* I did a large portion of my knee rehab at the trail heads, while David biked. It gave me motivation to keep working and I benefited from time in nature.

It's time to let that go for now. The plan did not go as you'd hoped, but it's done. It's over. You can't change what happened, so now you need to deal with where you are. Which could include allowing yourself to not only be open to other workouts, but to—*gasp*—enjoy them.

They aren't the same, and likely for a while, most won't get you anywhere near a runner's high, but begrudging them for not being running isn't doing you any favors. Start thinking about how they can help you become a better runner or just be open to trying all kinds of different workouts that you previously wouldn't have had time for. Occasionally, you might just find yourself genuinely appreciating the fatigue of new muscles, the camaraderie in a class, or an instructor whose perfectly timed words lift your spirits.

STEP 6: REMEMBER YOU'RE GOING TO BE OKAY.

I know I just said you could kick people with the trite words, but this one is really important. As you've started to work through those emotions, it's really key to latch on to the idea that you will get through this and you will find your way back to fitness.

Carrie Cheadle, a professor of sports psychology at John F. Kennedy University, makes an important point: "Emotional recovery isn't really linear. It cycles through denial, distress, determination, and often back to denial again. There are lots of highs and lows." See, once again, you've found that your healing process is very normal. And we want to work our way away from the lows and the crazy highs to find a spot in the middle where we can keep progressing through recovery to find our new normal. The middle just keeps winning.

7 LIES RUNNERS LOVE TELLING

We don't mean to lie per se, but we do tell ourselves things to make the process easier, and this might just give nonrunners the wrong idea.

1. **We never struggle with motivation.** Who doesn't want to pop out of bed before the sun to go sweat in the subzero feel of winter?

2. **Running always makes us feel good.** Can't run from those endorphins, even when you've got a bone sticking out of your thigh, just joy all around.

3. **Running is absolutely not why we're injured.** Heck no, it wasn't the 30-mile unnecessary training run over lava rocks that tore up our feet.

4. **We run to eat.** Did someone say pizza night? Better go run. Oh, time for birthday cake, better go run again. In fact, why not just keep running and eating simultaneously to save time?

5. **Weather doesn't factor into our decisions.** Hurricane happening? Whatever; we'll just layer up.

6. **I am never running a marathon again.** Fake news, sorry; I can't even pretend we mean this lie.

7. **You get used to the early mornings!** What do you mean you hate waking up in the middle of the night to get in your long run, it's just the most special time of day.

CHAPTER 4

DON'T PLAY THE INJURY GAME

"What if you can't run again?" This was the fear others loved to voice for me, in the months leading up to knee surgery. But that was never my fear, no matter how badly they wanted me to own it. It's like the nonrunner asking, "Did you win?" as though anything less made the race a weekend wasted.

No. I knew I would run again. I didn't see any other option. It wasn't just my passion, my joy, my release from the world; it was also my job. Over eight months of injury prior to surgery, I'd muddled through the daily nonstop running conversations, waving off any worries about my knee and doing what I'd learned through many marathon cycles, taking it a step at a time.

The real fear wasn't of never running again, it was of loving it less. Like that high school friend that you remember with fondness for going along with your horrendous idea to toilet paper a crush's house; you meet again and the memories are there, but the familiarity is gone. The time apart just can't quite be bridged.

For some runners, an injury forces them to once again appreciate every mile, but I'd been in love with those miles for years. As it turned out, knee surgery only reinvigorated my love for the sport as it allowed me, after seventeen years, to embrace being a beginner once again.

I remembered what it was like to enjoy each milestone without the pressure of what I'd done before. I danced a jig clicking register for my first postsurgery race because I knew it would be about crossing the finish line with my husband's hand held high and a megawatt smile, not at all about the clock. Running effortlessly isn't something I'll ever understand, but I have honed my skills at running with ease over thousands of miles and to feel it coming back was undeniable joy.

Whether you've been lucky enough to avoid injury, have suffered through the same injury repeatedly, or are now on the mend and dealing with the fear of hurting yourself again, this chapter has the tools you need to get through it.

LET'S TALK ABOUT OUR KNEES

I could start with a variety of common runner issues, but having just shared yet another story about me, I think our knees are an appropriate segue. This is where the naysayers will triumphantly pump their fist and shout, *"Aha, gotcha! Running is bad for your knees!"* Luckily, this is a book, so my eye rolling and passive-aggressive smile can't be seen, but I suppose pointing it out probably defeats all that.

Listen up, my pavement-pounding friend: your knees will not deteriorate from running.

Studies, as well as my very smart orthopedic surgeon, have confirmed there is no higher incidence of osteoarthritis in runners than in nonrunners. Running also lubricates your joints! Which means that it actually helps them to continue working better and with less pain. And more important, runners tend to have a higher bone density and overall better health than our less active counterparts.

What gives with the high rate of reported knee pain in runners?

1. Adaptation: Newer runners need time for their body to adapt to the stress of training. It's the same as feeling sore after lifting weights or jumping into a pickup softball game after ten years and waking up the next day unable to lift your arms.
2. Neglect: Longtime runners tend to neglect the cross-training that creates stronger hip, gluteal, and even back muscles because, quite frankly, we'd rather be running.
3. Sports Injuries: Active people put themselves in more situations where injuries are possible, whether that's in their given sport or from choosing a more active life (hello, whitewater rafting, hiking a volcano, sumo wrestling).

Running = pain or running = injury, is an incorrect belief system. You shouldn't be in pain and you really don't have to get injured. Let me demonstrate this radical idea by taking you back to my first real experience with a running injury.

As a young, know-nothing-whatsoever-about-marathon-training twenty-year-old, I could get away with mistakes in my training, a lot of mistakes, such as those mesh shorts rolled up at the waistband. And I did get away with a lot until shortly after my first marathon. With stars in my head and blue and yellow in my eyes, I set my sights on Boston Qualifying. I would do this by following the genius plan I mapped out for you previously. As you know, that resulted in debilitating IT band pain.

Then began the all-too-familiar runner injury cycle: I went to the doctor. I rested. I ran. It returned. Repeat ad nauseam, except throw in numerous temper tantrums, because I was frustrated and lacking endorphins. Unbeknownst to me, I was skipping over a fundamental step in the middle that could have eliminated the cycle. The sole focus among runners I knew was mileage; everything else was "nice to do," but who had the time for all that stuff?

What's important to know is that once I figured out this piece, I spent ten years running an average of 1,600 miles a year without more than a little twinge here and there that would prompt me to take an extra rest day. I learned how to deal with the random aches so quickly that I never needed much more than a day or two off to get right back into my training.

What's the secret?

1. Understanding that you don't need to run yourself down to progress
2. Realizing that running isn't the only way and heavy lifting isn't the only way and yoga isn't the only way. They're all tools to improve our fitness and combined make us better athletes.
3. Learning to strategically implement moves that I learned from highly respected physical therapists, elite runners, and other coaches

Turns out those "nice to dos" were actually must-dos. Instead of feeling overwhelmed by this section and sighing at the addition to your to-do list, use my method: **one change at a time**. You don't have to do everything at once, and honestly, shouldn't, because you're now catching on that too much, too soon, too fast, applies in lots of ways. Instead, start by adding one new thing to your routine. Slowly, it will become such a habit, you won't think twice about doing it, and then you can add on another piece of the puzzle until you've built yourself a nearly injury-proof body.*

In order of priority:

• Dynamic warm-up (covered in Chapter 7)
• Hip stability
• Hip strength
• Glute activation
• Core strength

---

* I'm just gonna put it out there that this is way better than a "beach body." Although, really, all these pieces could help with that goal, too.

- Mobility
- Flexibility
- Bonus: body care

You might not think strong hips are sexy now, but wait 'til we all come together for our BQ by 80 attempts. There will be some straight-up ogling at those with a full range of motion and some natural unreplaced hips keeping them running strong.

INTRODUCING PREHAB

Today, I'd like to introduce you to one of my favorite words: *prehab*. Prehab is why I didn't have any running injuries for over a decade after that IT band incident. If it weren't for a wild and crazy trampoline afternoon, I think my knee pain might have waited another decade to rear its ugly head.

Instead of waiting for an injury to occur, then spending months of time on rehab while quietly sobbing into our green smoothies, we can do a few things each day, right now, to prevent most injuries.

Before you start thinking about how little time you have, I want to assure you this is doable. It's broken down into key areas and you don't need to do everything at once. Rotating through these moves as part of your dynamic warm-up becomes an easy way to stay ahead of muscle imbalances and weaknesses that lead to pain.

And of course, we all know that with the proper motivation, we find time for things that matter. I mean, you magically find time for a weekend long run, but not so much to fix the drip in your master bathroom sink. Priorities.

THE MOST COMMON INJURIES

Speaking of motivation, how about not dealing with people smugly looking at you and saying, "*See, I told you running was hard on the body.*" Running is a natural motion for our body and why we do it so freely as children. The problem of course is that we start adulting. We stop running around, we sit all day, and then need to help our body get strong and flexible enough to do it again.

As with every sport, running can lead to injury. It's not the act of running that's generally the problem, it's that as runners we tend to want to do nothing else, skip the warm-up, skip the drills, what is this cross-training you speak of? In team sports, those things are woven into the daily practice, which helped us learn movement patterns and stick to the sometimes boring pieces of training.

Here are a few of the most common issues that lead to running injuries:

- Weak or tight hips
- Weak glutes
- Tight calves
- Building mileage too quickly
- Pushing speed too far too fast
- Poor running form

What you did not see on this list was running itself. You could throw out your arm from overuse in swimming, break a nose in volleyball, or need stitches from a line drive to your eyebrow with a softball (this may or may not have happened to my mom and, once again, I claim no responsibility).

Injuries happen, but we do have control over preventing three of the most common:

- Knee pain
- IT band syndrome
- Shin splints

If our goal is to run for many happy years, then it's time to rethink how we treat our runs. You don't just play a softball game without a warm-up. You practice catching fly balls, throwing to first base, throwing from the outfield, running while throwing . . . it's a whole thing, which I vividly recall from twelve years of postgame sodas. Without the team atmosphere and because we're busy, runners jump from bed into their shoes and out the door. Returning home, it's right into the shower, not a second spared on the cooldown stretching to aid flexibility.

Like many runners, I'm not a huge fan of spending hours in the gym. Each time I was given recovery exercises I would do them until I could run pain-free and then peter out because I would rather spend all my time running. As noted, this cycle leads to a roundabout of injury, recovery, repeat.

Finally, it hit me that these didn't need to be done as a separate sixty-minute gym workout. In fact, most of the exercises were perfect for a dynamic warm-up because they engage the glutes, loosen the hips, and warm up all muscles for a better run. That little shift took it from a burden to something that could easily become a habit because I could connect the benefit of the movements to my run.

That same mind-set is what helped me create a consistent weekly strength-training practice. Find the moves and the mentality that help you see the benefit to your run, and it's much easier to carve out time. Aha, there's that why and our fitness personality coming together again.

WHY HIP STRENGTH MATTERS TO RUNNERS

Although intuitively we know that our muscles are all connected, we tend to focus solely on the legs when we think about running. It's where pain appears, it's what's sore, and it's what we blame for most injuries.

In talking with a variety of physical therapists over the last decade, it's interesting to note that the majority of our common injuries stem from the hips. Slowly it has become more common knowledge among runners that we need to strengthen our hips and glutes, but I want you to understand why. Being told to do something is fine, but once you know how it's helping you, the motivation to stick with it long term is much higher.

Geeking out over the science of how our body moves isn't for everyone, so I'll keep this brief, but it's important to continue connecting the dots on how these moves benefit your runs.

Our hip muscles serve as the stabilizers for our body, and when weak, result in changes to movement patterns, which often causes overuse injuries. Here's how that might show up:

- Creates a tight IT band, which then begins to pull your kneecap the wrong direction
- Knee falling inward, instead of remaining in line with toes, when you run, creating knee pain
- Twisting when you run to compensate for tightness in the hips, creating knee pain
- Unstable pelvis, creating lower back pain
- Muscle imbalances
- Poor form when doing squats or lunges (now that cross-training we forced upon you is causing injuries)

Strengthening weak hips helps by repairing our movement patterns, allowing the appropriate muscles (e.g., your glutes) to take on the load of the workout, and providing more power to your stride.

UNDERSTANDING OUR HIPS AND GLUTES

Are you thinking of the hourglass figure or your Aunt Hilda's hip joint replacement? Most of us recognize that our pelvis creates the width of our hips, but minus the rare instance that a runner has a pelvic fracture, our actual "hip" focus tends to be on the surrounding muscles, tendons, and fascia.

Keeping the science to a minimum, here are the key players:

- **Hip flexors:** They allow you to raise the leg in front and when flexible to reach full extension for pushing off the ground to create momentum.
- **Adductors:** These muscles move the leg inward and across the body and are the primary driver in creating knee stability; this includes your groin and inner thigh.

- **Glutes:** Yes, the butt muscles are part of your hips! They control everything from moving your leg out to the side, to extension, to internal and external rotation of the leg.

Because a tight muscle can't function optimally, it becomes weaker over time, which means we need to incorporate both strength and stretching to harness the full power of our hips. A good example of this is runners who find themselves with consistently tight hamstrings, though they spend plenty of time stretching. In this case, the lack of glute and hip strength is sending signals to the brain that the hamstrings need to fire to compensate and keep your run going, which leads them to become overworked and feeling tight.

A number of studies have proven that strengthening weak hips is more effective at relieving knee pain than focusing on improving knee function, which means incorporating these exercises is going to keep your knees happy for many years to come.* Before jumping into the exercises, let's first talk about the glutes, because they work together with the hips for optimal power.

WHAT ABOUT ENGAGING THE GLUTES?

When we talk about the gluteal area, it's not just one large muscle, but three: the gluteal medius, maximus, and minimus. Working all three is required to keep us running strong. Unfortunately, the majority of exercises tend to focus on the maximus to give you that Kim Kardashian booty. Of course, I want you to have a lovely bum you can be proud of in your spandex, but mostly I want you to have a derriere that functions like a beast when you're out running.

There are two main problems that occur with regard to our lazy bums:

---

* Bonus motivation from a 2005 study in the *Journal of Strength and Conditioning*, which showed that improving hip flexor strength decreased run time by up to 9 percent. That seems like a pretty solid payoff for a few minutes before or after a run.

INHIBITED GLUTES

In this scenario, we're talking about glute muscles that simply are not firing. Whether it's standing up from a chair at work or trying to push the pace in a hill workout, when they don't fully activate, the body relies on other muscles to pick up the slack, which is not only inefficient, but entirely unfair. Think of it like when you have a group project, but only one of you stays up all night to finish the work. You're so exhausted you miss your alarm and the project gets turned in late despite your hard work. Wah, wah, wah.

OVERSHADOWED GLUTES

In this case, the glutes are working, but not at full force. They're turned on but not engaged, so to speak. Like when you showed up for work, but didn't actually hear anything that your boss said for the last ten minutes. It results in poor performance and frustration all around.

Whenever you perform a movement, such as a squat, lunge, deadlift, jump, sprint, or any exercise that involves several different muscle groups, the majority of work should be handled by the strongest of those muscle groups.

Basically, these two different definitions allow you to see that there is a spectrum of lazy backsides. Sometimes your glutes will initially fire, but stop as you get into harder movement patterns, whereas other times, they simply aren't kicking in at all and in both cases are holding you back.

GLUTE ACTIVATION TESTS

Not sure whether your glutes are firing or taking a nap? You can try these quick glute activation tests to find out what's firing and what needs some extra work! Of course, you'll always learn more from going to a physical therapist,* but these are things you can do at home.

---

* You might think I'm being paid by the Board of Physical Therapists to send you there, since I keep mentioning it. But I don't even know whether that exists and I'm really only

Test number one: squeeze your butt cheeks together as hard as you can. Congratulations; we have confirmed you have glute muscles and they can be worked. Now, let's find out exactly what level of engagement you have under that spandex.

COOK HIP LIFT

Lying on your back, place both feet on the floor, knees bent. Pull your right knee into your chest and place a tennis ball or small physical therapy ball in the crease between your quad and pelvis. So, now you have one foot on the floor and one knee pulled in toward your chest. Release your hands from your right knee, and push your left heel into the ground, slightly raising your hips. The movement might only be an inch or two, but you should actually feel the glutes contracting on the left side.

The ball will force you to focus on the glutes, because going too high starts using your back muscles and the ball will fall. *Don't* drop the ball, literally.

SINGLE-LEG ACTIVATION

The single-leg test most commonly prescribed states that you should be able to stand on one foot with your eyes closed for sixty seconds. Each time I've tried this, my motion sickness kicks in and I need to vomit before sixty seconds, which I assume is not a sign of weak glutes, but maybe a weak mind?!

---

trying to save you hours of frustration when you find yourself injured because you didn't fix poor form, movement, or weaknesses when you had the chance.

Instead, I prefer the single-leg stability ball test. Lie on your back with your legs straight on a stability ball. Engage your core and glutes to raise into a hip bridge. Lift your right leg straight into the air, leaving only your left heel on the ball. Using your left leg, pull the ball toward your bum, while keeping your hips high. Aim for 10 reps and repeat on the other side. If you can't complete 10 reps, that's a good sign that you need extra strength work or a quick way to see whether one side is stronger than the other. If you find that one side is weaker, complete the following exercises on both sides, but add a couple more reps to the weak side.

GLUTE AND HIP ACTIVATION EXERCISES

How do you activate your glutes? By including a number of glute-strengthening exercises that force them to fire through isolation and get them reengaged. As with every single physical therapy move, the key is to work these into your existing running routine.

Include a couple of these as part of your running warm-up; then you're consistently activating your glutes and strengthening your hips, rather than trying to remember to add an entirely new workout to your schedule. If you're doing this as part of your dynamic warm-up, I recommend picking five or so each day and doing 10 to 15 reps per leg. For a complete stand-alone workout or as part of a strength-training day, do at least two rounds of 10 to 15 reps.

Clamshells (Forward and Reverse)
A standard clamshell is lying on your side with knees bent at 90 degrees. While keeping your ankles together, raise your top knee, as if opening a clamshell, and you should feel the activation in your hips and glutes.

Don't stop with that standard move; embrace the time on the floor. Add a reverse clamshell, where you keep your knees together and raise your top foot. This is often overlooked, but allows you to activate the muscle in a different way for maximum impact.

To ensure that your glutes are firing and not just your hips taking over, get into the same position, but with your feet on the wall. Push that top foot into the wall as you raise its knee to do the clamshell; you won't raise it as high, but should feel more action in your glutes.

BULGARIAN GOAT BELLY LIFT

Standing with the butt of a kettlebell pressed into your core, think about tightening your abs and then hinge forward from the waist, creating an L shape from your upper body to lower body. The bending is slow, but the return to standing is a quick powerful movement. This is a unique but effective way to force your entire core to work together and fire up your glutes.

WALL PRESS ACTIVATION

Facing away from the wall, bend one leg to 90 degrees and press the heel of your foot into the wall. Hold this for 20 to 30 seconds and repeat on the other side. This is not a stretch; it's a static contraction to activate your muscles.

BANDED WALKS

This is another commonly prescribed physical therapy move that has stuck with me for years because you can always feel it working. Place a looped band around your ankles and lower into a half squat. While keeping tension on the band at all times, walk 10 steps to the right, 10 left, 10 forward, and 10 backward. You may find you need to angle your feet in just slightly to maintain tension and keep your knees from dipping in.

SINGLE-LEG EXTENSION WITH STABILITY BALL

Standing on your right leg, bend your left leg as though pulling it back for a quad stretch and place your foot on top of a stability ball. The ball should be just behind you with both legs still aligned, your left knee pointing toward the floor.

Then, you will begin to bend your right knee while extending your left leg behind you. The stability ball under your left foot will force you to engage your core and should feel like a good hip flexor stretch as you fully extend the left leg. Once extended, engage that left hip flexor to pull the ball back in and return to standing with your foot remaining on the top of the ball.

STABILITY BALL ROTATION

In a tabletop position with your knees on the ball and your hands on the ground, rotate both knees to the left and then pull yourself back to the starting position. Repeat going the other direction for a full rep. You'll need to engage your core and hips to make this move work, otherwise you'll be slip-sliding right off the ball onto your bum.

STABILITY BALL HIP BRIDGE

Lying on the floor with both heels on the stability ball, fully extend your legs and raise your bum to create a straight line from head to toe. Then, focus on using your glutes to pull the stability ball toward you, while keeping your core tight and high. At no point will your bum move toward the ground; you'll remain in that reverse-style plank from start to finish of the movement.

BEYOND STRENGTH TO FLEXIBILITY

In addition to strength, our hips need to be flexible. Part of what can cause muscle inhibition is tightness from other muscles. This is one reason your friends swear by yoga and we keep forcing you to engage with that torture device known as the foam roller.

While I was growing up, it was an ongoing family joke that I couldn't touch my toes. I'm not sure why it was so funny, but for me it was kind of humiliating. My long-ass legs grew too fast for my upper body and no one talked to me about stretching, so once a year I'd do the Presidential Fitness Test and feel like a ridiculous failure. But now, I can place both hands on the ground and a lot of my peers can't touch their knees, so who's laughing now. That flexibility didn't happen overnight, but just like my running, was a process of slowly and consistently sticking to a routine.

Stretching, whether through a yoga practice or at-home moves, will loosen your hip flexors to help resolve misaligned pelvis or rotational pelvis issues (e.g., when you find one leg is longer than the other). Sitting causes the hip flexors to remain flexed and active all day long, which results in overuse and then stiffness. Our goal is to help resolve that along with a variety of other causes, such as running itself, which shorten and tighten our muscles.

Static stretches are always meant to be done after your run, or in my case, at the end of the day when I'm watching yet another detective solve yet another home invasion gone wrong. Don't get frustrated or toss it out because you can't stretch immediately postrun. Ensure you walk for a bit to cool down and then stretch when it fits in your schedule; just make it happen.

These stretches are meant to be held for up to one minute per side. This is not something to rush; rather, to slow down and make part of your routine. A chance to embrace slow as a good thing.

DEEP SQUAT

Unlike doing a squat for a body-weight workout, in this stretch, you want to sink down and settle in to stay. With your knees slightly wider than your hips and your toes pointed slightly outward, lower down until your bum is next to the ground. Work your way up to staying here for at least 1 minute and keeping your heels on the ground throughout the pose.

If you have trouble getting into or staying in the squat, it's best to start out by holding a bar for stability or placing a rolled-up mat under your heels. Keep your head and chest up! The goal is to allow your lower back to relax and let go.

CHILD'S POSE

Much like the deep squat, child's pose is another release for your lower back and your brain; something about it forces you to relax! There are two options for child's pose. The first is to place your feet together, knees out wide, and then lower your upper body to the floor. The second option is to place your feet and knees together, then fold your body over your quads. Each will give you a slightly different stretch, so you may find that one simply feels better to you.

ASSISTED QUAD STRETCH

Facing away from a wall or couch, sit on your knees and scoot back until you have both feet pressed against the wall. Now, go into a tabletop position, bending your right leg and scooting back to press your shin against the wall. From here, you'll take your left leg to 90 degrees and then straighten your torso. It will look like the old-school standing quad stretch you've seen so many times. Keep your body tall and straight; don't lean back or forward. The more flexible you get, the closer you'll be able to get that right knee to the wall, deepening the stretching.

After holding for 30 seconds to 1 minute, switch sides. The assisted quad stretch is more effective due to the added resistance and mobility it creates throughout your entire hip joint.

KNEE HUG

Who couldn't use a hug every day?! Lying on your back with both legs straight, bring one knee to your chest, wrapping your arms around it and holding. Keep your other leg straight on the floor for another static stretch to release your low back.

FORWARD FOLD

Standing tall with your shoulders back, roll forward and allow your hands and head to hang down. This stretch is all about bending from the waist and not just curving your back. Hold, and with a deep breath, see whether you can fold a little farther.

FIGURE FOUR

Lying on your back with both feet on the floor, pull your right knee in toward your chest, while crossing your left ankle over your right knee (hence the figure four). With your hands behind your right leg, pull in toward your chest until you feel the stretch in your left hip.

There's an endless variety of stretches, so look for the ones that feel good to you. That slight tension as you get into the move is a great sign you're working into a tight area. Personally, I could sit in cobbler's pose or pigeon pose for the duration of a great Kardashian fight.

GETTING YOUR BODY INTO ALIGNMENT

All the hip strength and stretching in the world won't fix a body that is out of alignment. When your hips are shifted, it creates a situation where one leg is longer than the other or your pelvis might be tilted forward or back, altering your stride. That misalignment of your spine creates tension in other areas of the body, which leads to the tightness, pulling, or compensations that create pain.

A chiropractor with a focus on athletes is an invaluable tool in your recovery kit. This professional can identify muscle imbalances or joint restrictions to keep you running smoothly. If you consider the amount of pounding your body takes to put in mile after mile, it makes sense that your body could potentially shift or need some help getting back into alignment.

If you are too nervous to go to a chiropractor or worried that once you go, you must go forever, hey, I get it. I watched my dad go as a kid and refused to go for many years because I thought that then I'd need it constantly as well. That's not how it works. If you do the exercises here, the muscle strength and flexibility will allow you to maintain that alignment longer. The pounding of running does shift your body and make it likely you won't simply go once and be done for life.

It's a bit more like massage. I don't need it in the sense that I'm going to starve without it, but oh man, does my body feel better if once a month I allow someone to dig into my calves so hard it brings tears to my eyes.

Hip Alignment

I talked about weak hips and glutes that have abandoned you, but how do you know whether your body is functioning on a squiggle rather than a straight line? Would you be surprised to know I found a few tests you can do at home to determine whether your hips might be out of alignment and causing issues? You're welcome.

- Compare your left and right sides: Is it harder to balance on one side? Is one side weaker, more painful, tighter, or stiffer? If any of this is true, your pelvis may be rotated.
- Lie on your back, bring your knees to your chest, and then slowly stretch them straight on the floor or against a wall. Ask a running buddy to see whether one leg is longer than the other (*I can often*

tell this on my own with legs up the wall). Your friend can do this by holding a broomstick or other rod across your feet, then across your hip bones in front and back when you're standing. Most often, the right hip bone appears to be higher than the left one, if the pelvis is rotated.

After being assessed or seen by a chiropractor, here are a few at-home exercises to help continue creating hip strength to prevent pelvic rotation. These should be done in conjunction with the hip stretches and glute exercises shared here. As always, I am not a doctor and you should consult one before starting any routine, but I have found these to be helpful for myself.

For each of these moves, I'll describe them on one side, but you should perform them on both sides. I feel quite certain that goes without saying, but wouldn't want to shortchange you. Try to perform each move ten times and, as noted previously, you can do three rounds for a stand-alone program or incorporate a few of these for one round into your warm-up.

ISOMETRIC HOLD LEGS

Lie on your back with both legs on the ground, then bend your right leg to 90 degrees.

Place your hands around the back of your thigh, creating light resistance, and push away with your leg for 10 seconds, repeating 10 times.

Place your hands on the front of your thigh, creating light resistance, and push your leg toward your chest for 10 seconds, repeating 10 times.

ISOMETRIC HOLD HIPS

Sit on the floor with both knees pulled in toward your chest, feet together.

Wrap your arms around your legs, with the crook of your elbow just below your knee.

Push your knees outward with all the force you can, while resisting with your arms.

Hold for 30 seconds and then invert.

Place your elbows inside your knees, pushing out with your arms and in with your knees.

90/90 HIP ROTATION

Lying on your back with your feet on the floor and your knees bent at 90 degrees, place a block or pillow in between your knees.

Begin to drop your knees to the right, keeping both shoulders on the ground. If your shoulder comes up, you have gone too far.

Return to center and rotate to the left without letting that block fall; repeat 10 times per side.

SCORPION STRETCH

Lie on your stomach with arms stretched out to form a T.

Moving slowly, lift your left leg in the air, bending at the knee, and rotate it across the midline of your body, touching the ground near the right side of your body. The goal is to work toward keeping your shoulders on the ground.

Come back to resting and repeat on the opposite side.

As noted, please don't be overwhelmed by everything that I've shared in this chapter. Instead, turn down the page like a good little reader, set this next to your foam roller, and then make a habit of picking out a couple of moves to do before each run or on your recovery day when I know you're doing all the mobility work, right?*

WHAT ABOUT RUNNING FORM?

What kind of running coach would I be if I didn't tell you to fix your running form? I mean, we built a whole industry of barefoot running around the idea that none of us knows how to run properly. It's clearly a massive topic. But is it, really?

What we now understand is tinkering too much with your natural stride leads to awkwardness, decreased enjoyment of running, slowing

---

* I know I didn't even get into mobility in this book, but Google it, or better yet, head to RunToTheFinish.com and find out how to do it and why. Shameless plug and I don't feel bad about it one iota.

down, and, interestingly, other injuries. Which is why, my little snow-flake, I am not here to change you.

But I do want to make you better where possible and I want you to shine bright like a diamond. Which is why I quite cleverly (can you say that about yourself) developed the acronym STAR to indicate the areas we can all focus on for better form:

SHOULDERS DOWN

I know this running is serious business, but I checked and having your shoulders pulled up to your ears does not in fact improve your run. In-stead, you've created tension that radiates down your back, into your hips, which can mess with your stride. Yes, it's that the-whole-body-is-all-connected thing at play once again.

This is usually my first indicator that I'm way too worked up about a race or writing a book. Take a few deep breaths, consciously allow your shoulders to drop and roll back just a bit. Hold your chest out like you're wearing a great big Superman *S* and need to show it off.

TORSO UP

Have you ever noticed when you pass a runner who is struggling hard-core during a race, that person tends to be hunched over? We're tired and our body is trying to think of ways to conserve energy, but the more we allow ourselves to slouch, the less oxygen we can take into our lungs. Less oxygen, less energy, less energy, less motivation—really, it's a spiral we don't want to get into.

Instead, think of being pulled up by a string through the top of your head and focusing your eyes straight ahead. You'll often be surprised at how that posture shift suddenly makes you feel more energized. It's a bit like getting into power pose before a big meeting.

ARMS FORWARD

Forward sounds obvious, yet all too often I spy runners with arms flailing out to the sides (we call those chicken wings), or worse yet, sawing back and forth across the front of their body. Each time I see this, I want to rush over, tackle the runners, and tell them they aren't allowed to begin again until we resolve this.

Why? Your goal is to move forward, but now a portion of your energy is swaying side to side, which is a horrible waste. Worse yet, your arms crossing your body leads to torso twisting, which leads to pain in your hips, knees, and feet because the whole body is now counteracting itself. "Do you want me to go forward or sideways?" it wonders.

The arms are undervalued for their importance in running. These are motors that help dictate the pace of your feet, give you extra power on the uphill when you swing upward like a punch, and can remind you to release tension when you focus on a soft grip, not a fist. Your arms should be at a 90-degree angle, pumping forward and back. Your hands should be palms facing in and attempting to hold a potato chip without crushing it between your thumb and forefinger.

REVOLUTIONS 180

This is possibly the hardest one, and yet I promise, with a little practice you'll find it becomes very natural. One thing the barefoot movement did an incredible job of shedding light on, besides the unbelievable Tarahumara, was the prevalence of heel striking and how that jars the body through, creating a breakinglike motion. Our natural inclination is to try to lengthen our stride, reaching to cover more ground, but this is wasted energy and bad form.

Instead, we want to focus on shorter, quicker strides and we do that through the optimal foot turnover of 90 footfalls per side, per minute. The best way to gauge your current rpm is to count each time your right foot hits the ground for 10 seconds.

(Right footfalls for 10 seconds x 2) x 6 = total footfalls in 1 minute

The goal of 180 will be the same whether you share my 33-inch inseam or are closer in height to Desi Linden. Those quicker, lighter steps help to reduce overall impact on the body and appear to be the most efficient cadence for conserving energy.

You can learn this technique by loading a Spotify playlist with a 180-beat track on your phone and practicing matching your feet to the beat. Elite distance runners to middle-of-the-packers all use this stride rate, so it's not about pace. However, increasing your rate from 150 to 180 might just be the ticket to helping you speed up.

All right, my newfound STAR, grab your shoes and head to Hollywood.

INTERESTING RUNNING FACTS EVERY
RUNNER SHOULD KNOW

The marathon was not an event of the ancient Olympic games. The marathon started in 1896 in Athens, a race from Marathon—northeast of Athens—to the Olympic Stadium, a distance of 42.195 kilometers.

Fifty-nine percent of race participants are now female.

The fastest mile ever run: Hicham El Guerrouj from Morocco in 3:43:13 and Svetlana Masterkova of Russia in 4:12:56.

Forty-five degrees is the optimal race day temperature, based on scientific testing of how the body reacts to different temps.

Researchers from the University of Portsmouth in England found that breasts don't just bounce up and down during running; they move in a **complicated figure-8 pattern** and, without support, could create saggy breasts!

The foot has 26 bones, 33 joints, 112 ligaments.

Your neighborhood cat can run faster than a human!

It takes **200 muscles** to take a step when you run.

Average finish time across all 2015 Boston Marathon finishers was 3:46.

CHAPTER 5

DREAMING JUST BIG ENOUGH

Before exploring training plans and all the new exciting things you'll be doing to stay injury-free, let's talk about big, hairy goals. Can I perhaps help you avoid my folly of chasing a goal with reckless abandon? Looking for it to happen overnight, rather than over the years?

Most elite marathon runners have been training for close to a decade, and some much longer, before winning their first big race. It's not because they don't want it sooner; rather, the body takes time to adapt to the continued stresses of training to be strong enough to achieve our goals. And so does the mind. Throughout those years, they have races where they show an incredible burst of growth and others that could appear to be a step back.

Yet, they continue to persevere because it's never about one race. And that's the mind-set we're adopting here: trusting that with each choice, we're building a body that can withstand thousands of miles and a mind that can enjoy those miles without a fixation on the watch. It's easy to get caught up in each individual run as we try so hard to follow each specific run on a training plan, but it's the sum of your training that truly matters.

Knowing that, how do you pick a goal that's right for you, right now, where you are? First, we'll talk about pace, then about setting your sights on the marathon, or not.

CHOOSING A GOAL PACE

While I don't believe that the clock should be our only motivation, it doesn't mean that improving our runs can't still be a fun part of running. Once again, it comes back to mind-set: knowing that *your* goal pace is perfect for you and doesn't need to be compared with anyone else's.

It's about enjoying the work to reach that new level of fitness . . . embracing the fact that you can push yourself and knowing that even if you don't get all the way there, you can be tremendously proud of the progress you made along the way. Not only that, but each bit of work means you're still moving toward the goal; it may simply take longer than you'd originally planned. Remember those elite runners and keep focusing on the long run.

Figuring out your goal pace can be tricky. We often have a dream goal pace based on comparisons, a realistic goal pace based on not fully believing we can achieve more, and a pace somewhere in the middle that we should shoot for to push our boundaries without breaking our body.

Here's the process I use while coaching to help determine a goal pace that's motivating and just enough of a stretch to feel like a win on race day.*

STEP 1: EVALUATE YOUR TIMELINE.

The first thing to consider when picking your new goal is your timeline. Have you gotten inspired for a 10K that's a mere thirty days in the future? You can certainly see some progress, but not a ton in four weeks. Especially if you want to train smart and for the long haul.

---

* Have you started to notice that I really love putting things into steps or lists? It's because I want actionable advice when I read a book or go to a conference. Hopefully, that's exactly what you're finding here!

How long do you need to train for a race? Here are some standard ideas based on new runners:

RACE	DISTANCE	WEEKS
5K	3.1 miles	10 weeks
10K	6.2 miles	12 weeks
Half marathon	13.1 miles	18 weeks
Marathon	26.2 miles	24 weeks

Times could be less for each distance, depending on how many years you've been running, your current weekly mileage, and any history of injuries. Without a coach, it's up to you not to rush the process in a frenzy to have that medal around your neck.

After all, why rush it? Enjoy the buildup, the weekly progress, and the anticipation of race day. There are so many moments to celebrate; don't shortchange the training with an eye on nothing but the finish. Especially because we all know that one finish simply leads to registering for the next start line.

Once you've evaluated your timeline, you'll have a better idea of how much you can expect to progress prior to race day. Don't be like the Amanda of 2007; be smarter and focus on consistent progress, not a massive leap over the course of one training cycle.

STEP 2: REVIEW THE RACE COURSE.

Do you examine the course before registering? Or do you, like me, pick a great vacation spot and then excitedly proclaim you'll be running a race there? I love that approach, but you have to set your expectations to match a course that's a net downhill at sea level or one that's through the hills of elevation in Colorado.

- The best way to PR is a consistent pace from start to finish (yup, better than negative splitting!).
- A superhilly course means you'll need to plan for pace adjustments.

- A course with lots of turns means you'll be slowing down and speeding up repeatedly.
- Compare this course to those you've done previously and how they affected your time.
- Review potential weather conditions; you will slow down in the heat or possibly just hate running in the cold.

Courses love to proclaim they have rolling hills or beautiful scenery, which might be true from a car but feel a little different on foot. Check out the elevation profile and the course map to get an accurate view of what you'll be tackling. Then, you'll know whether you should treat this as a great practice race, fun run, or a place to hit a new personal best.

STEP 3: BALANCE BIG DREAMS AND REALISTIC EXPECTATIONS.

Not to be a buzzkill on your own Boston Qualifying dreams, but realistic pace goals are essential to the right training paces, staying injury-free, and having a race that you can celebrate.

It's not always easy to pinpoint a goal pace because a lot of factors come into play.

- New runners will often see massive gains in pace from one race to the next.
- Longtime runners might have a massive PR by shaving a minute off their time.
- Do you have time to increase your mileage? Cross-train?
- Are you open to trying a running group, which might give you a little competitive push?
- Are you focused on quality recovery and nutrition?

Find a recent per-mile race pace and then compare it to your goal race pace. If you're looking to shave minutes off every single mile, you need to review the previous questions and decide whether you're being too pie-in-the-sky or realistic, based on the fact that you didn't train as hard last time, were brand new, or possibly were injured.

STEP 4: SET A RACE PACE GOAL.

Finally, we have reached the long-awaited section of actually figuring out at what pace you want to run each mile. You know the course, you've committed, you're excited, but how do you choose a race pace? We have a few more things to evaluate, which will help you get to that ideal goal.

Evaluate Your Current Fitness

Be honest with yourself about your current running. Have you been doing it? Do you have a recent race time to judge your fitness? Plug that data into a race pace calculator to get an initial idea, and then consider how that output compares to what you've actually run previously. These calculators are about 50/50 when it comes to accurate race predictions, so put your faith in what you know more than what it says.

Consider Your Running History

Newer runners can often expect a much bigger jump in improvement levels because they're learning and adjusting, whereas longtime runners have dialed in much of what works for them already. Additionally, if you have a tendency to get injured, that's going to impact the intensity and duration you can handle to push toward a big PR. Being injury prone could be a result of skipping the prehab and other pieces discussed throughout this book. Perhaps dialing in those areas will allow you to begin a more intense training plan, but again, take it race by race.

Repeat Test Runs

Find a route you regularly run from 3 to 6 miles depending on your goal, and every five weeks, use that run for a speed workout. Start by warming up for a mile and then push yourself to that race day feeling, which is a perceived exertion of a 7 to 8 for most distance runs. Keep an ongoing record of your progress to determine whether you're on track for the big goal you set.

Race Pace Miles

For some reason, very few training plans include race pace miles, but it's one of the best ways throughout training to find out whether you're on track. Early in training, you might be able to hit a few miles, but shouldn't expect to run a long way at your goal pace. Instead, these miles are saved for later in training when you have built a solid foundation. Start to sprinkle them into long runs or as part of your midweek long run. It will not only help you see how you're progressing, but teach your body exactly what it feels like to hit your goal pace.

STEP 5: RUN PRACTICE RACES.

You know what's a fabulous way to take the pressure off a race? Call it a practice race. Suddenly, you're no longer focused on the clock, but instead on testing yourself and learning more about your limits. This is an ideal way to get better information than the online calculator can provide, while improving your fitness and your knowledge for the goal race.

When you're pushing to a new goal like the sub-two-hour half marathon or even building up to your first marathon, practice races are an incredible opportunity to improve sans pressure, and I've seen many result in incredible PR performances. Although, that is not to be expected.

A practice race could be a shorter race woven into your training plan as a speed workday or it could be a replica of your goal distance. This is easier to achieve with distances shorter than the marathon where the recovery time needed after the race is less. However, longtime runners may choose to do a practice marathon in the spring then take those lessons through summer training to nail their big goal in the fall.

Practice races are a chance to do more than think about the finish line or your watch. The goal is to *learn* as much as you can to improve the odds of your goal race going well.

- How did you feel at the start line? Do you need more throwaway clothes to stay comfy?
- Do you need to be awake longer to digest and use the bathroom?

- Were you superstressed getting to the start line? Can you stay closer next time?
- Was a destination race harder for you because of the travel?
- Do you like being surrounded by others for energy or find that draining?
- Did music cause you to go out too fast? Maybe start it later in the race as your energy drops.
- Did that gel make your stomach hurt? Would you do better with whole food fuel?

ENJOYING THE EXPERIENCE

We're so tense on race day that we often forget this is supposed to be fun, and worse than that, we waste boatloads of energy that could be going to our legs by scrunching up our face to concentrate or tightening our shoulders. A practice race means you have absolutely zero pressure to perform, so you can practice the art of enjoying race day.

PRACTICE PACING

Although you are *not* going out for a PR, this race is a good chance to see how it feels when you push your limits. Did you find your energy waning by mile 10 because you rocketed off the start line? Did you finish still thinking you had something left to give?

Notice your breathing, your legs, the tension in your shoulders, and yes, whether you were even having fun. Learning to ride that fine line of pushing, but not too far, takes experience, and you'll only get that through toeing the line. But not every race can be an A race where you push it to the limit. Even elites only do this a few times a year, so why should we expect more from our body?

COURSE EVALUATION

Pay attention to how hills, turns, or a tightly packed group of runners played with your pace. Do you actually need to start a little farther forward to avoid dodging slower runners? Do you enjoy the hills because of the changing muscles you use? Do you love hearing screaming crowds or enjoy the silent stretches where you could get in the zone?

Practice doesn't make perfect, but it does help untangle some nerves and give us tools to continue our forward progress.

SHOULD YOU RUN A MARATHON? SHOULD ANYONE?!

Now that we've explored some thoughts on pace and practicing along the way, let's discuss the marathon. I've heard more times than I can count that "*I haven't run a marathon, so I'm not a real runner*" or "*I just want to cross it off my bucket list.*" A is invalid and B is okay if you know what you're in for.

A few months each fall, hundreds of marathons take place, making it feel like every runner you know is doing 26.2, including some of the big attention-getters, New York or Chicago. It seeps into our psyche. We want that glory of crossing that 26.2 finish line, of shouting from the rooftops that we're a freaking marathon finisher.

Of course, those finish lines don't tell you the story of what it took to get there. The tears runners shed at mile 23 as every muscle in their body began throwing an epic two-year-old-style tantrum that it Would. Not. Go. On. The moment an inflatable dinosaur passed them and they suddenly found the courage to continue pushing onward.

Want the real skinny on what training is like? See my No BS marathon training truths on page 133.

Having completed eight marathons, I admit there's an indescribable sense of accomplishment that comes with the finish line. But I can also tell you there have been many more years when I opted not to train for or run a marathon because I understood what it required and that it didn't define me as a runner.

Before you get swept away with the idea of 26.2, please consider my reasons not to run a marathon as your guide to deciding whether it's really right for you.

Don't Run a Marathon Because You Think That It's a Requirement to Be a Runner.

If you run, you are in fact a runner. A real runner isn't about pace or distance; it's a mind-set. *Amanda, we freaking get it, we're runners.* Okay, cool, just as long as we're all on the same page, I'll move on and try not to mention the whole real runner thing again.

But seriously, you don't need to run 26.2 miles to be a runner. Have you ever tried racing a single mile full out?! My respect for short-distance speed runners is off the charts.

Don't Run a Marathon If You Don't Want To.

It's a lot of work if you don't already enjoy running a half marathon. Friends have said that having a second child isn't twice as much work, it's triple the work. I'm pretty sure the marathon is a similar endeavor. It's not just twice the distance, it's a whole new ballgame of training and mileage.

If you're only doing this for a friend or because it's on a life list, the training isn't going to be all that enjoyable, and race day is likely to be even less fun because you've probably skipped a bunch of training. Marathons are an experience for which you need to be in the right mind-set to wholeheartedly embrace the early mornings, weird new workouts, aches, needing bigger shoes,* and the emotional roller coaster of race day.

Don't Run a Marathon to Lose Weight.

The unfortunate truth is that most first-time marathon trainees gain weight. This happens for two very good reasons. First, the body sees all the energy being expended as new and different, so it increases your hunger levels to ensure that you aren't going into starvation mode. Second, you justify those delicious ooey-gooey fresh-from-the-oven cookies based on your new mileage.

---

* True story, most distance runners wear a full-size-larger shoe than they used to wear. Mostly because our feet swell over the long miles, but I'm pretty sure our feet also grow from the pounding, like pizza dough. But don't quote me on that.

Can you lose weight while training for a marathon? Yes, but there are a lot of ways that are easier.

DON'T RUN A MARATHON IF YOU NEED TO HAVE PRETTY FEET FOR A PHOTO SHOOT.

I've never lost a toenail, but I'm one of the lucky few. I do, however, have calluses and blisters. And honestly, in general, a lot of marathon training just isn't glamorous. It's looking exhausted after your first 18-mile run, but showing up to help a friend shop for her wedding dress. It's compression socks under your work pants and walking sideways down stairs after a race because it hurts to go any other way.

DON'T RUN A MARATHON IF YOU HAVE TO ASK SOMEONE "HOW LONG IS *THIS* MARATHON?"

Of course it's your first and maybe you're new to running, so you'll have plenty of questions. But you need to have enough running history to have a concept of 26.2 miles. Try driving it; often, that's all it takes to terrify me into realizing just how far I've agreed to run. Let's add to this that if you're still saying you ran a 5K marathon last weekend, you aren't ready.

DON'T RUN A MARATHON IF YOUR SOCIAL LIFE IS KEY TO YOUR HAPPINESS AND NONE OF YOUR FRIENDS RUN.

It becomes harder as the miles grow to go out for late night fun when your Saturday is going to start at five a.m.! Additionally, you are going to *talk* about running nonstop and need people who won't throttle you for it. No joke; it's why I started blogging in 2005! I thought my husband would explode if I spent another night regaling him with the details of my first-ever 17-mile run, but I was so psyched I needed someone to talk to. Enter the Internet.

DON'T RUN A MARATHON IF YOU'RE HAVING HEALTH ISSUES. IT WON'T MAKE THEM BETTER.

Marathon training can weaken your immune system without the right plan, coach, and nutrition. And unfortunately, most of us don't grab a coach for our first; we wing it, which can so often lead to overtraining, underfueling, or other issues. Although running can help you lose weight, get stronger, and strengthen your cardiovascular system, if you have adrenal fatigue or other major issues, this just isn't the time.

DON'T RUN A MARATHON IF YOU'RE ALREADY OVERCOMMITTED IN OTHER AREAS OF YOUR LIFE.

It takes time to train for a marathon in a way that ensures you don't get injured, which is to say you'll need hours not only for the weekend long runs, but the body care that goes in between. Much of which we covered in Chapter 4, but also includes getting a little more sleep than normal, maybe scheduling in massages and chiropractor visits and extra time to talk about your training with other runners, because what's the point if no one knows how hard you're working.

Busy people train for marathons all the time, so it's not impossible, but really look at your life and be honest about how much time you can and want to give to running right now. Tips for managing it all are covered later in this chapter.

DON'T RUN A MARATHON IF YOU DON'T ENJOY RUNNING!

Similar to many others, I didn't love running right from the get-go, but clearly now I can't live without it. *Fall* in love with running before you choose to go after the marathon distance. This might seem like an obvious statement, yet you'd be surprised at the number of people who say they hate running, but want to run a marathon. It's the allure of the challenge and the mystique of something that seems so out of reach, which becomes far less exciting at four a.m. on Saturday.

Of course, the flipside are the reasons that we run marathons and why I've still got my sights set on a few more 26.2 finish lines.

- Pride in an epic achievement (less than 0.5% of the United States has run a marathon!)
- Discovering a new level of determination
- Creating an inner belief system that we can handle hard things

- Experiencing new places (why all my marathons are race vacations)
- Finding a community that embraces us regardless of pace
- Because we really do love the run

Still not sure whether you're doing a marathon for the right reasons or that now is the time? I love actionable advice, so here's a cut-and-dried checklist to help you make the final decision:

- You have enough time to devote to weekend long runs (3+ hours if you count the warm-up, cooldown, shower, and refuel).
- You have been running long enough to average injury-free at least 20 miles per week.
- You have a good why to keep you going when training gets hard, because it will absolutely get hard.
- You have a training plan that's realistic for your life and current level of fitness (e.g., no jumping from 20 miles per week to 40 miles with tons of speed).
- You're excited for the experience of training and growing, not just that shiny medal.

Once you can say yes to most of these, it's time to buy another pair of your favorite running shoes, hit register, and start training. And if you're not quite there yet, then keep right on enjoying the thrill of chasing new half marathon goals or testing your skills in the 5K.

HOW TO TRAIN WHEN YOU'RE CRAZY BUSY, WITHOUT LOSING YOUR MIND

You've gone through the list and decided a marathon makes sense for you, but who has the time?! Well, honestly, I probably have more time than the average person since I work from home, running is my job, and I have no little people needing their nose wiped.

Choosing to be a distance runner already puts you in the category of being just a little bonkers, but we don't want it to push you all the way over the edge. Instead, let's talk about how you can work in all the miles with your current juggling act of volunteering at Girls on the Run, writing supertechnical work documents, and devouring homemade pizza Fridays.

What we prioritize we make time for, which means that if you've decided a marathon is in your future, you need to figure out how to make it a priority for a little while. No fretting over daily balance needed.

1. DEDICATE TIME AND MAKE A DAILY COMMITMENT.

Maybe you love the *idea* of running a marathon, but your current work and family obligations already have you feeling frenzied. Instead of overbooking yourself, take a hard look at your choices and commit only to things you can truly give 100 percent. If you don't, it's a surefire way to find yourself skipping out on runs.

If you aren't ready to commit to the training schedule, don't beat yourself up—readjust your current plan. Maybe you can squeeze in enough workouts to train for a 5K or 10K. Even though these are shorter races, having a more attainable goal will keep you committed to the runs, and you can use these to build up to a marathon when you *do* have the time.

2. PLAN TO WIN.

There's a reason the quote "If you fail to plan, you are planning to fail" is so popular. If you don't take the time to plan and commit to your running schedule, chances are, you'll let life get in the way. This goes beyond having a training plan; make sure to take additional steps to head off any obstacles:

- Mark your workouts in your calendar to have the time already blocked off (account for change time and travel time if going to a gym).

- Keep a gym bag in your car or at your desk with running clothes, so you're always ready.
- Know your travel/weekend schedule and shift workouts to accommodate other plans if something comes up.
- Schedule time with friends when it won't impede getting your run done (but do schedule it!).

3. SAVOR YOUR REST DAYS.

If you're one of the dedicated runners who feels a rest day is simply a waste of good energy, remember you can use that day to do other things and think of it as a reset for the following week. It's time for your body to heal, to plan your training and meals, and treat yourself to some well-earned relaxation.

If you just can't sit still, why not try a nonrunning way to get your body moving? Maybe spend some time hiking, paddle boarding, or going on a bike ride with friends and family. Days when you aren't training allow you free time with those whose support ultimately makes you a stronger runner.

4. HAVE AN ACCOUNTABILITY PARTNER.

Being part of a running group can make your runs more interesting, encourage you to push your pace, and get you more involved in the entire running community. But having a single running partner can be even more beneficial. Imagining him or her standing on a corner as the sun rises, waiting for you to appear is the ultimate way to make sure you don't hit Snooze a second time.

5. EMBRACE MORNING RUNS.

I know you probably groaned just reading this tip, but it's true. The busier your life, the easier it is to skip a run later in the day. There are the rare few who will *always* run, even if the only time they have to spare is late at night, but if you tell yourself you'll run after work and then don't, it's time to embrace the mornings.

Studies show that morning runners are more productive and make healthier choices throughout the rest of the day. I think it's the endorphins, but maybe it's because they've started their day by enjoying the world before everyone has woken up and the noise of life has truly begun.

If, after all this, you still can't seem to make yourself run, I'd say it's time to consider you've hit burnout. Explore some new activities, and once the urge to run sneaks up on you again, grab it by the laces and go.

Even a perfect round of training is no guarantee of a great race day. Nerves, travel, eating fried catfish the night before (*yup, I've done that*), weather, can all derail our best laid plans. You can probably guess what I'm going to say next. You've got to get your mind right around a good or a bad race.

Once again, we're back to the idea that as runners we need to embrace practice. Repetition is what makes things feel less scary and boosts our confidence on race day knowing exactly how our body will react and what works best for us.

In Chapter 10, we'll dive more into how to harness those race day nerves and everything else to make it the best possible experience.

WEIRD THOUGHTS WE ALL HAVE AT THE START LINE

1. Why is my GPS signal so awful? I hope it picks up before the race starts. What if it doesn't, what will I do? I can't start it, like, midway through.

2. Why are the Porta Potty lines so long and didn't I just go? I think I need to go again . . . better get in line.

3. I don't remember them saying it would be so ___ cold, hot, windy, any variation of not perfect weather.

4. God, that guy looks really fast; maybe I should move back. I'm not really interested in getting run over today.

5. Hmm, I should totally be able to beat her . . . I wonder how many people I'm going to have to dodge; should I move up? I mean, I really want to PR.

6. Okay, remember I paid to do this, it's supposed to be fun, or at least I'm finishing because I *paid* to do this.

7. Are we moving? Did they say something? I can't hear . . . oh, never mind; they haven't done anything yet.

8. I hope I ate enough, I think I'm hungry . . . no, I think I'm nauseous. No, hungry . . . no. . . . can't we just start?!

9. Hope I see my family on the course. Wonder if they made signs? Are they wearing the bright shirts I told them about; what if it's so busy I miss them?!

CHAPTER 6

THE PERFECT TRAINING PLAN

The perfect training plan is like the perfect diet. If one program worked for everyone, it wouldn't be a billion-dollar industry. We'd all eat the same foods, fast food would likely not exist (which makes me fear for the fate of pizza), and we might all have six-pack abs, so what would be the point of Instagram.

Running follows a general formula, just like eat more veggies, eat fewer of those delicious Hot Tamales and Snickers bars. You need to build your mileage slow and steady, work on total body strength and stability to prevent injuries, then add speed in the appropriate amount and intensity.

The exact makeup of how that looks on a spreadsheet color coded by day can vary wildly. Not just because some runners need a 6:1 run/walk setup, whereas others are cruising through a six-minute mile on a tempo run.

A great training plan for the half marathon, marathon, 10K, 5K, and all the other distances floating around needs to account for lifestyle, injury history, what you enjoy about running, and your honest goals.

Honest goals? That's right, time to get real with yourself about the goals you've been writing down. No more flip-floppery or telling yourself it's a goal you should be chasing.

Early on, I shared my IT band injury story, which came from trying to Boston Qualify because everyone else was set on doing it. My heart wasn't in it, so when I leaped forward on that journey, it wasn't with a smart plan or even enjoyment of the plan. Which is incredibly common because we can so easily compare ourselves at running groups or via social media.

Not all comparisons are bad. They can help us consider goals we never realized were possible or they make us want to work harder. But when we find ourselves chasing a goal that really doesn't spark joy, it must be placed in the donation pile per Marie Kondo.*

Are you truly excited for intense weekly track workouts to reach that massive PR? Do you really want to spend your weekends doing back-to-back double-digit runs for an ultramarathon? Are you ready to implement a dedicated recovery plan?

Maybe you're fist pumping, eyes ablaze, thinking, "*Yes, I can't freaking wait.*" But maybe you're not. Perhaps what you want is a bit simpler: to enjoy training, showing up injury-free on race day, and having a darn good run. With your honest goals in mind, you can start to choose a plan that's right for you. Otherwise, you're on a path to burnout, boredom, injury, or frustration.

We're here for the long haul, not a single race.

We're here for miles and miles of smiles.

We're here to achieve our goals both PR and non-PR alike.

---

* In case you're reading this many, many years after publication and missed this craze, Marie Kondo inspired us all to clear the clutter from our homes and led to thrift stores being overrun with donations. As a self-proclaimed minimalist, the idea sent fear through my family's heart because they thought I'd get rid of the few things I had left.

HOW TO SELECT THE RIGHT MARATHON TRAINING PLAN FOR YOU

Which brings us to the wide whacky world of training plans. One friend Boston Qualified by maxing out at a 16-mile-long run, and others with three 22-milers. How the heck does this happen? There are a variety of different plans because we all have different needs.

While you don't have to love every second of pushing through a hard workout to get to your shiny new PR, you need to enjoy the majority of the process. That PR moment is short-lived; the training is long and we don't have to do it. It's true, right? No one is forcing you out the door to run. Except maybe a spouse who has realized you're far more pleasant after some stress-relieving miles.

Beyond what's working for your friends or what you've seen people on Instagram raving about this week, it's important to know yourself and what really works for you. We found a way to love the run, so why lose that joy over a few minutes in one race?

- Do you thrive on hard track workouts? Or do you dread them nonstop?
- Do you have time for lots of long runs or need to make workouts quick and dirty?
- Do you want plenty of time for cross-training?
- Do you prioritize strength over time running?
- What's your training timeline?
- What's your current running ability?
- Are you enjoying running right now?
- Are you feeling energized or run down?
- How did past training cycles leave you feeling?
- Do you find yourself consistently injured during a certain part of training?
- Do you know what easy and hard efforts should feel like?

Although many run coaches wouldn't go down the rabbit hole of asking what type of workouts you enjoy because they believe there is a best way, that's not me. If you aren't enjoying the training process, then why suffer through eighteen-plus weeks of it? Beyond that, I have coached people in nearly all of these methods and they've all PR'ed, which means you can make any plan work to your physical and mental strengths.

Now that you know the factors involved, let's go deeper into what each of the most popular training methods includes. Being able to compare them in the following pages will help you figure out what feels like the right fit. Because there are many books on each one, this isn't an exhaustive dissection; rather, it's an overview for comparison.

The key is to find one style and stick with it for the duration of training. Too often, we get excited about one idea, pulled into another as we train with friends, and suddenly our miles, our intensity, and our purpose are all over the place.

Training plans are designed with a very specific progression to build your base, your strength, your speed, your maximum mileage, and your taper to race week. But each plan does it differently and you could be negating the benefits by trying to throw in too many variables.

CLASSICAL MARATHON PLAN—HAL HIGDON

You can assume that 90 percent of the free training plans you find online are based upon the classical style of marathon training. Derived by Hal Higdon, or Greg McMillan, these plans generally included five runs per week, with one of those being a long run up to 22 miles, one speed workout, and limited cross-training.

Classical marathon training plans became popular with the boom of jogging,* a time when people who were no longer elite runners started showing up to race as a hobby. Even then, the majority of marathon

---

* This is not a jab. It's the terminology they actually used at the time, though we all know they were runners.

finishers were sub-four hours and it was still a sport enjoyed by a small population. These were some of the first plans to introduce the idea of periodized training: flowing from a base-building phase into speed workouts, peak mileage, and then taper. Along with that, they had a built-in rest day and followed a consistent formula, making it an easy place to start with training.

On sites like HalHigdon.com, you can find a variety of free plans. Although these plans still work, I think some of the others reviewed here have adapted more to the wider variety of runners, goals, and lifestyles involved in training.

	MONDAY	TUESDAY	WEDNESDAY	THURSDAY	FRIDAY	SATURDAY	SUNDAY
Week 11	Cross-train	5 miles	8 miles	5 miles	Rest	8 miles	18 miles

From the Intermediate 1 Plan

WHO SHOULD TRY IT?

A classical marathon plan is a great place for most runners to start figuring out mileage, how to build in a smart way, and what the process is going to look like.

The major downside is that very little cross-training is noted or recommended, which you're starting to understand from this book is key to staying injury-free and running longer. If you select one of these plans, it will be up to you to incorporate those workouts, usually on speed run days, to ensure you are getting enough recovery other days.

GALLOWAY METHOD—RUN-WALK

Are you a newer runner taking on your first marathon? Are you someone who is still working to increase your endurance? Are you someone training in wicked heat/humidity and need to keep your heart rate from shooting straight through the roof? That last one, I learned while living in Miami, where nearly every runner embraced this training method from the twelve-minute milers to the seven-minute Boston Qualifying runners.

According to Jeff Galloway, the one who popularized the run-walk method, "Walk breaks will significantly speed up recovery because there is less damage to repair. The early walk breaks erase fatigue, and the later walk breaks will reduce or eliminate overuse muscle breakdown."

Important to note this is not the walk-once-you-get-tired method, this is the run-walk-the-entire-time method to help prevent that feeling of fatigue. During walk breaks, your body creates endorphins that allow you both mentally and physically to recover, allowing you to build your endurance without breaking down your body. Although Galloway is certainly not the first to utilize run-walk, he has made it popular and structured, allowing many people to run farther and/or faster. Here are some keys to this method:

- Every run is a combination of a run interval followed by a walk interval and repeat.
- Interspersing intervals of walking and running, you can avoid injury and fatigue.
- Don't split up the long run—it's about practicing time on your feet.
- Doesn't promote cross-training, except aqua jogging
- Very little speed work

Many runners find themselves needing to walk as they increase their distance, but without a set structure once they start walking, it's often hard to get started again. This eliminates the thinking and puts you on a specific schedule to keep you going.

The run-walk ratio guideline as provided by Galloway is in minutes (run:walk) unless otherwise noted. The run-walk intervals will change as you decide what feels best for you. Many runners start with the 1:1 ratio and move all the way to 8:1.

8 min/mi—4:35 sec

9 min/mi—4:1

10 min/mi—3:1

11 min/mi—2:30:1

12 min/mi—2:1

13 min/mi—1:1

14 min/mi—30 sec:30 sec

15 min/mi—30 sec:45 sec

16 min/mi—30 sec:60 sec

These are not strict numbers, but a general idea to get you started. Find the ratio that feels best to you in terms of a rhythm, while still creating sufficient recovery.

	MONDAY	TUESDAY	WEDNESDAY	THURSDAY	FRIDAY	SATURDAY	SUNDAY
Week 11	Rest	30-minute run	Rest	30-minute run	Easy walk	Rest	10.5 miles

Train to Finish plan

WHO SHOULD TRY IT?
The Galloway method is fantastic for runners who are looking to increase their endurance, but struggling to do so or simply feeling nervous about the jump. You can continually modify the duration of run-to-walk intervals as you progress, and the overall plan will guide you through the right amount of mileage to finish the race feeling strong.

HANSON METHOD—HARD RUNNING

Do you love high-fiving your friends after a set of 800s at the track? Do you enjoy that feeling of red-lining it through the final miles of a race? This might just be the training plan for you, as it's based on overall intensity.

The Hanson Method operates on the idea that by running more miles during the week, you are in essence running on tired legs for your weekend long run. You will build more mental and physical endurance by consistently running in that fatigued state. Which sounds horrendous to me, but has worked well for many of my friends.

Following are the key concepts of the Hanson Method:

- High mileage
- Six days of running
- Speed emphasis early in the training plan
- No cross-training
- Cumulative fatigue—"The development of fatigue through the long-term effects of training which results in a profound increase in running strength"
- Three SOS (something of substance) workouts per week: speed work, tempo run at goal race pace, and long run
- Longest run is 16 miles for most people.

How did they come up with the idea of a 16-mile-long run? It's all about the percentage of total miles for the week. In many programs, the long run can consist of up to 50 percent of the runner's mileage and thus requires more time to recover and potential for injury.

> Too little of a long run and you don't
> stimulate the proper adaptations. Too long
> of a run and you have to take too much time
> to recover from one singular training run.
> This takes away from other valuable training
> before and after the long run.
>
> —Luke Humphrey

	MONDAY	TUESDAY	WEDNESDAY	THURSDAY	FRIDAY	SATURDAY	SUNDAY
Week 11	6 miles	Speed workout	Rest (or strength)	Marathon pace 8 miles	6 miles	8 miles	10 miles

WHO SHOULD TRY IT?

The Hanson Method is ideal for runners who thrive on speed training or have found that the 20- to 22-mile-long runs often leave them injured. It's rarely a plan that I would recommend for first-time marathon runners, except those who are crushing the half marathon already and want to use that speed to build.

MAFFETONE METHOD—LOW HEART RATE

The Maffetone method (named for creator Phil Maffetone) has gained popularity in recent years, but is probably not one that a lot of runners have heard about. However, because this is the method that I've been using for at least five years, I want to explain it. If you're familiar with my website, you've heard lots about it, but for everyone else, let me introduce it.

Low-heart-rate training is absolutely not for everyone, but for anyone who has issues with high cortisol (hello, lots of stress), hormonal issues, fatigue, health issues . . . well, it's a pretty spectacular way to keep your body happy while continuing to enjoy the runs you love.

The MAF method (also known as maximum aerobic function) in regard to running is pretty basic, which makes most people assume they've missed something . . . they haven't.

- No run should be done above your max calculated heart rate.
- The first mile should be done up to 10 beats per minute slower than max.
- *All* cardiovascular work should be done at or below this number.
- A MAF 3- to 5-mile test is performed every 4 weeks to monitor progress.
- **This is NOT training in heart rate zones.**
- After plateauing, you can add some speed, but no more than 20% of weekly time.

The goal is to improve speed while maintaining the heart rate, which is most efficient for utilizing fat as fuel, recovery, and overall bodily stress.

	MONDAY	TUESDAY	WEDNESDAY	THURSDAY	FRIDAY	SATURDAY	SUNDAY
Week 11	Recovery	4 miles	Cross-training	10 miles	Full-body strength	3 miles	18 miles

WHO SHOULD TRY IT?

This training method will work for runners who enjoy long, easy-feeling runs, and especially for runners who find themselves consistently run down as training goes along. It will not work for those who love speed workouts or thrive in classes like Orangetheory.

FIRST (FURMAN INSTITUTE OF RUNNING AND SCIENTIFIC TRAINING) PLAN

Billed as an ideal way for runners to prepare for their first marathon **running only three days a week,** this program requires a focus on training intensity to achieve the best results. It was created by Bill Pierce and Scott Murr as they began triathlon training and found that time/energy wasn't available to complete the standard long weekly mileage of most plans.

The two discovered that running three days a week allowed them to maintain fitness. Further studies and work with athletes led to the full FIRST program, which they believe is an optimal mix of hard running and cross-training to achieve optimal results.

- "Less Is More"—run only 3 times per week.
- Pacing is based on a current 10K time.
- Three key workouts per week: tempo, speed intervals, long run
- Cross-train at high intensity.
- Pace specific workouts to improve VO_2max and build fitness.
- Long runs are done at or close to goal marathon pace.

On nonrunning days, you should be doing cross-training from cardio to strength sessions. You will not be heading out with friends for an easy chat-away-the-miles kind of run. Each run will have a purpose and intensity to it.

	MONDAY	TUESDAY	WEDNESDAY	THURSDAY	FRIDAY	SATURDAY	SUNDAY
Week 11	Cross-training 30–35 minutes	10–20-minute warm-up 1 mile (400m RI), 2 miles (800m RI), 2 x 800 (400m RI) 10-minute cooldown	Cross-training 30–35 minutes	2 miles easy, 3 miles @ tempo pace, 2 miles easy	Rest	Distance: 16 miles Pace: PMP + 30–45 sec./mile	Cross-training 30–35 minutes

WHO SHOULD TRY IT?

Those who are short on time and not injury prone might find this is an ideal way to train for a race. It's also a great option for those who want to do other sports or don't love running, but really want to finish a marathon.

COMMON TRAINING-PLAN QUESTIONS

The best thing about hiring a running coach is not just someone to keep you accountable. It's someone who can adjust your plan throughout training to keep you feeling strong, help you when you've missed five days because someone sneezed on you and suddenly you were bedbound, or add clamshells to your warm-up because you've been noticing some hip issues.

Contrary to what I believed for so many years as a new runner, coaches aren't just for the über-fast. In fact, they're often more valuable when you're starting out and have no clue what to do when you miss a long run or freak out over that race week calf tightness.

But since you may not have a coach, let's see whether I can do some mind reading to answer your top training-plan issues.

CAN I CHANGE AROUND THE DAYS FOR MY SCHEDULE?

Yes. But you need to configure them with the same amount of time between hard workouts. If you're going to skip one of the planned training days entirely every week, then try to make it an easy day and factor that into your goal.

IF I MISS A RUN, DO I MAKE IT UP?

Rarely.

IF I'M FEELING REALLY GOOD, CAN I DO SPEED WORK ON AN EASY DAY?

Sometimes, our body feels awful; sometimes, we just want to let it rip. I fully believe in letting your body take the lead, so go for it and push hard. If you're going to push it, don't fall in that gray zone of being not really hard and not easy enough to be a recovery run. Go hard or stick to the planned easy workout. Afterward, adjust your plan by making the next hard workout an easy one or moving things around so you aren't doing back-to-back intense runs.

WHAT IS CONSIDERED CROSS-TRAINING?

Every training plan is a little different, so I'd say, look into the book on whatever you have chosen to follow. But ideally, you'll be doing at least two strength-training sessions each week, which can be body-weight focused and don't need to be hours long!

In terms of the best cardio cross-training, that depends on what you enjoy. But there are benefits to most options:

- Biking at 90 rpm mimics the ideal foot turnover for running.
- Swimming will increase your lung capacity and provide low-impact workout for recovery.
- Rowing builds your upper body strength for power on hills.
- Pilates will build core strength, provide a strength workout, and increase flexibility.

More on all cross-training options in Chapter 7.

WHAT CAN I DO WHILE INJURED?

Something—you can almost always do something! During my knee injury and following surgery, I focused on tons of upper body and core workouts to keep me sane. When there wasn't pain, I took easy walks, I embraced the bike, and kept finding ways to move.

Assume that a thirty-minute run is equivalent to a sixty-minute bike ride, and really focus on playing with intensity on the bike, too. Keep your easy days long and steady, but do tabatas or sprints on days you would have had a speed session.

In the pool, you can search for a local place with an underwater treadmill, or you can get a waist belt that helps you aqua jog in the deep end and then swim laps. Don't let an injury stop you; let it be your tool to develop new strengths to keep moving forward.

MY PERFECT TRAINING PLAN

Having told you previously that you need to find what works best for you, I was loath to set a training plan in digital ink. But many discussions on social media later, I realized that you're smart enough to use this as a guideline and adjust it to meet your needs.

Also, it wasn't until I began pulling all these together that I realized most standard training styles are named after a running coach. Suddenly the Brooks training plan had a nice ring to it.*

Following are four training plans:

---

* These may also be referred to as Run to the Finish plans because our main goal is to get from point A to point B without injury, with less pain, and a big ol' smile.

- Half Marathon Beginner (running your first or feeling you need to build)
- Half Marathon Intermediate (anyone shooting for sub-two and beyond)
- Marathon Beginner (running your first or feeling you need to build a more solid foundation)
- Marathon Intermediate (anyone shooting for sub-four and beyond)

While I'm sure some who are reading this are Boston Qualifying fast already and could follow something even more advanced, this book is for the middle and right now those stand among the few, the proud, and the brave. I may have borrowed that slogan from somewhere, but you get it.

Following tables are details for any specific listed workouts.

HALF MARATHON BEGINNER

This plan is best for anyone who is just starting out, recovering from an injury, or looking to build a really strong running base for continued healthy running.

WEEK	MONDAY	TUESDAY	WEDNESDAY	THURSDAY	FRIDAY	SATURDAY	SUNDAY	TOTAL
1	Recovery	3 miles + hills 1	30-minute cross-training or full body strength	3 miles + hills 1	Full-body strength	30-minute cross-training or rest	5 miles	11
2	Recovery	3 miles + hills 2	Full-body strength	3 miles + hills 1	Full-body strength	30-minute cross-training or rest	6 miles	12
3	Recovery	3 miles + hills 1	20 min cross-training + full-body strength	3 miles	Full-body strength	2 miles	7 miles	15
4	Recovery	3 miles + hills 2	20 min cross-training + full-body strength	4 miles	Full-body strength	2 miles	8 miles	17
5	Recovery	4 miles	Full-body strength	3 miles	Full-body strength	3 miles or rest	5 miles	15
6	Recovery	4 miles with speed play 1, 1 round	4 miles + core workout	30-minute cross-training	Full-body strength	3 miles	9 miles	20
7	Recovery	3 miles + upper body/core	5 miles: fartleks 5 x 1 minute	3 miles	Full-body strength	3 miles	10 miles	24

WEEK	MONDAY	TUESDAY	WEDNESDAY	THURSDAY	FRIDAY	SATURDAY	SUNDAY	TOTAL
8	Recovery	4 miles + upper body/core	3 miles + hills 2	30-minute cross-training	Full-body strength	5 miles	8 miles	20
9	Recovery	3 miles	6 miles + fartleks 10 x 30 seconds	4 miles	Full-body strength	3 miles	10 miles	26
10	Recovery	5 miles + upper body/core	6 miles	4 miles	Full-body strength	3 miles	11 miles	29
11	Rest	3 miles	Core workout, stretch	1-mile warm-up: speed play 1 round 1-mile cooldown	Recovery—mobility	3 miles	7 miles	16
12	Rest	3 miles with 5 x 20 seconds hard effort	Yoga, core, or rest	3 miles with 3 x 30 seconds hard effort	Rest—easy 1-mile shakeout	RACE DAY	Recover like a champ	20.1

HALF MARATHON INTERMEDIATE

This plan is best for those looking to crack the Sub–Two-Hour Half Marathon goal or faster. It's ideal to have a solid base of running behind you to prevent any overuse injuries.

WEEK	MONDAY	TUESDAY	WEDNESDAY	THURSDAY	FRIDAY	SATURDAY	SUNDAY	TOTAL
1	Recovery	3 miles + hills 1	5 miles + core workout	3 miles + hills 1	30-minute strength or rest	3 miles	6 miles	20
2	Recovery	3 miles + hills 2	5 miles + upper body/core workout	3 miles + hills 1	30-minute strength or rest	3 miles: 1 easy 1 GHMP 1 easy	8 miles	22
3	Recovery	3 miles + upper body/core workout	6 miles—speed play 1 x 1	3 miles	30-minute strength or rest	3 miles	9 miles progression	24
4	Recovery	5 miles + hills 2	Cross-training or easy 3 + full-body strength	4 miles—fartleks 5 x 1 minute	Full-body strength or rest	4 miles	10 miles: 2 warm-up 2 GHMP 2 easy 2 HMP 2 easy	26
5	Recovery	4 miles + full-body strength	6 miles + fartleks 6 x 1 minute	30 min cross-train	Rest	3 miles	8 miles	21

WEEK	MONDAY	TUESDAY	WEDNESDAY	THURSDAY	FRIDAY	SATURDAY	SUNDAY	TOTAL
6	Recovery	5 miles + hills 1	4 miles + full-body strength	5 miles: speed play 2	30 min strength or rest	3 miles	11 miles: middle 4 miles at GHMP	28
7	Recovery	4 miles + full-body strength	6 miles: fartleks 5 x 2 minutes	4 miles	Full-body strength or rest	4 miles	12 miles: last 2 miles hard effort	30
8	Recovery	4 miles + full-body strength	7 miles: 2 mile warm-up, 3 miles GHMP, 2 mile cooldown	5 miles	Full-body strength or rest	4 miles	13 miles	33
9	Recovery	3 miles	5 miles + hills 2	Full body strength	Rest	3 miles	9 miles: last two miles hard effort	20
10	Recovery	5 miles + upper-body/core workout	8 miles: progression	4 miles	Full-body strength or rest	3 miles	15 miles	35
11	Rest	3 miles + core workout	1 mile warm-up: speed play 1 round, 1-mile cool down	5 miles	Full-body strength or rest	3 miles	8 miles	22
12	Rest	5 miles with 5 x 20 seconds hard effort	Yoga, core, or rest	3 miles with 3 x 30 hard effort	Rest—1-mile shakeout	RACE DAY	Recover like a champ	20.1

* In this plan, it's optional to add in 30 minutes of cardio on Friday strength-training days.

MARATHON BEGINNER

This plan is designed to help you cross the finish line of that very first marathon, feeling healthy and supremely proud of your achievement.

WEEK	MONDAY	TUESDAY	WEDNESDAY	THURSDAY	FRIDAY	SATURDAY	SUNDAY	TOTAL
1	Recovery	3 miles + hills 1 + core workout	3 miles or cross-training	3 miles + hills 1	Full-body strength	3 miles	8 miles	20
2	Recovery	3 miles + hills 2 + core workout	3 miles or cross-training	3 miles + hills 1	Full-body strength	3 miles	9 miles	21
3	Recovery	3 miles + strength workout	5 miles—speed play 1 x 1	3 miles or 30-minute cross-train	Full-body strength	3 miles	10 miles	24
4	Recovery	5 miles + hills 2	3 miles + full-body strength	4 miles—with 1 mile at HMP	Full-body strength	4 miles	8 miles	24
5	Recovery	4 miles + full-body strength	5 miles	4 miles + hills 2	Full-body strength	3 miles	11 miles	27
6	Recovery	4 miles + full-body strength	5 miles—middle 2 miles at HMP	3 miles or 30-minute cross-train	Full-body strength	4 miles	12 miles	28
7	Recovery	5 miles + full-body strength	4 miles—fartleks 10 x 30 seconds hard effort	4 miles	Full-body strength	4 miles	13 miles	30

WEEK	MONDAY	TUESDAY	WEDNESDAY	THURSDAY	FRIDAY	SATURDAY	SUNDAY	TOTAL
8	Rest	3 miles + full-body strength	4 miles	50-minute cross-training	Full-body strength	4 miles	10 miles	21
9	Recovery	5 miles + full-body strength	6 miles	4 miles + hills 1	Full-body strength	4 miles	15 miles	34
10	Recovery	5 miles + full-body strength	7 miles: include 3 x 5 minute 10K pace with 3-minute recovery	4 miles easy or 50-minute cross-train	Full-body strength	3 miles	16 miles	35
11	Recovery	4 miles + full-body strength	8 miles—speed play 1 x 3	5 miles	Full-body strength	3 miles	17 miles	37
12	Recovery	3 miles + full-body strength	5 miles easy	4 miles easy or 50-minute cross-train	Full-body strength	5 miles	10 miles	27
13	Recovery	4 miles + full-body strength	9 miles—include fartleks 10 x 1 minute hard	4 miles	Full-body strength	3 miles	18 miles	38
14	Rest	4 miles + full-body strength	8 miles—include 3 x 10 minutes at HMP	5 miles	Stretching, core	3 miles	20 miles	40
15	Rest	3 miles easy	4 miles with 1 mile at HMP	3 miles easy	Rest	3 miles	8 miles	21
16	Rest	3 miles with 5 x 20 seconds hard effort	Yoga, core, or rest	3 miles with 3 x 30 hard effort	Rest—1-mile shakeout	RACE DAY	Recover like a champ	

MARATHON INTERMEDIATE

This plan is still not designed for the elite runners in our midst. This is for the middle of the pack who have completed a previous marathon and are looking to step up their game a bit.

WEEK	MONDAY	TUESDAY	WEDNESDAY	THURSDAY	FRIDAY	SATURDAY	SUNDAY	TOTAL
1	Recovery	3 miles + hills 1 + full-body strength	5 miles	3 miles + hills 1	Full-body strength	3 miles	10 miles	24
2	Recovery	3 miles + hills 2 + full-body strength	6 miles	4 miles	Full-body strength	3 miles	9 miles: middle 2 miles at GRP	25
3	Recovery	3 miles + full-body strength	6 miles—speed play 1 x 2	4 miles	Full-body strength	3 miles	12 miles	28
4	Recovery	5 miles + hills 2	3 miles + full-body strength	4 miles—with 1 mile at HMP	Full-body strength	4 miles	13 miles	29
5	Recovery	4 miles + full-body strength	7 miles	4 miles + hills 2	Full-body strength	3 miles	15 miles	33
6	Recovery	4 miles + full-body strength	5 miles—middle 2 miles at HMP	Full-body strength	30-minute cross-train	4 miles	10-mile progression run, last mile faster than GRP	23
7	Recovery	5 miles + full-body strength	4 miles—fartleks 7 x 30 seconds hard effort	5 miles	Full-body strength	4 miles: middle mile at GRP	17 miles	35

WEEK	MONDAY	TUESDAY	WEDNESDAY	THURSDAY	FRIDAY	SATURDAY	SUNDAY	TOTAL
8	Rest	3 miles + full-body strength	8 miles	4 miles: 1-mile warm-up, 3 at GRP	Full-body strength	4 miles	18 miles	37
9	Recovery	5 miles + full-body strength	6 miles: speed play 2 x 1	4 miles	Full-body strength	4 miles	20 miles	39
10	Recovery	3 miles + full-body strength	7 miles: include 4 x 3 minute HMP pace with 3-minute recovery	4 miles	Full-body strength	3 miles	16 miles: 2-mile warm-up, then alternate easy mile and harder mile	33
11	Recovery	4 miles + full-body strength	8 miles: speed play 1 x 3	5 miles	Full-body strength	3 miles	18 miles	38
12	Recovery	5 miles + full-body strength	10 miles	Full-body strength	30-minute cross-train or rest	5 miles	20 miles	40
13	Recovery	4 miles + full-body strength	9 miles—include fartleks 10 x 1 minute hard	Recovery	Full-body strength	3 miles	16 miles: final 2 miles goal pace	32
14	Rest	4 miles + full-body strength	8-mile progression run	5 miles	Stretching, core	3 miles	22 miles	42
15	Rest	3 miles	4 miles with 1 mile at HMP	3 miles + 5 strides	Rest	3 miles	8–10 miles	21–23
16	Rest	3 miles with 5 x 20 seconds hard effort	Yoga, core, or rest	3 miles with 3 x 30 hard effort	Rest—1-mile shakeout	RACE DAY	Recover like a champ	

WORKOUT DETAILS

Here are specific workouts as noted in these plans.

Easy: Unless otherwise noted, miles should be done at an easy pace, which is to say a pace where you could comfortably hold a long conversation or, on a perceived exertion scale of 1 to 10, stay around a 4 or below. Assume a distance race day effort might get to around an 8 and an all-out sprint, well, we're distance runners, so that's not happening here.

Recovery: This could mean you take a full rest day to recuperate, or it could be the perfect day for mobility, stretching, restorative yoga, or an easy walk.

Strength: If you can do your Friday strength on Thursday with the run, that's ideal to give you another full recovery day. Focus on using dumbbells to help with core engagement, and lots of moves using a stability ball or standing on a single leg. You'll find more specifics and ideas in the following chapter.

Hills 1: Find a nearby steep incline or, on the treadmill, use 7%.

Do this at the end of your run.

5 x 10 seconds hard effort uphill

Recover walking down, allow body to fully recover before next repeat.

Hills 2: Find a nearby steep incline or, on the treadmill, use 7%

Do this at the end of your run.

8 x 20 seconds hard effort uphill

Recover walking down, allow body to fully recover before next repeat.

Speed Play 1: Done after you've warmed up for at least 1 mile at an easy pace. This is to help you begin feeling out the effort level different paces require, so you aren't always checking your watch. Complete the cycle the number of times indicated.

3 minutes moderate effort, 3 minutes recovery run

2 minutes harder effort, 2 minutes recovery run

1 minute hardest effort, 1 minute recovery run

Speed Play 2: Done after you've warmed up for at least 1 mile at an easy pace.

1 mile at previous race pace (PRP)

5-minute recovery

1/2 mile at goal race pace (GRP)

5-minute recovery

1/2 mile at 10K pace

5-minute recovery

1/2 mile at 5K pace

Fartleks: Unstructured speed plays. You'll pick up the pace for the reps and time noted, but without following a specific run/recovery cycle. You might do 1 minute, then recover 5 or recover 3, whatever feels good.

The pace will be a push, but not a sprint by any means.

Progression: This is not a start-slow-and-speed-up-really-soon run. Imagine running on the treadmill and simply bumping the pace up 0.1 each mile. It's a very slow build, with the first few miles focused on a nice easy pace, then finishing close to your goal race pace.

Now, find an old-fashioned ink cartridge and print out your Run to the Finish plan, thumbtack it to the wall, and give yourself a gold star for each workout you complete.

NO BS MARATHON TRAINING TRUTHS

1. You'll be bone tired on Mondays and still bragging at work about how great your training is going.

2. Your significant other will be very, very . . . very tired of hearing about your training (it's why social media exists).

3. You will suddenly have more foam rollers than underwear (which is cool because all your shorts have built-in liners so you need way less).

4. You'll always be planning your next meal (especially as runger strikes).

5. You will develop an inner knowing that you can do hard things.

6. Nonrunners will constantly exclaim either, "I could never do that" or "Oh, I ran a marathon last weekend," which you'll learn means a 5K.

7. You'll choose work clothes that allow you to slip on compression socks or wear flats.

8. Checking the weather will become your second job and regardless of what it says, you'll still run.

9. Time to think will allow you to solve world hunger and then promptly forget the solution when you get home and your bladder needs the bathroom.

10. A seventy-year-old will pass you, a mom with a jogging stroller will pass you, and you'll realize how amazing it is that running is available to everyone.

11. You'll talk more about bathroom habits than you ever planned and your running friends won't mind at all.

CHAPTER 7

WHAT IS SOLID TRAINING?

Solid: Used to describe something or someone as being superior, or excellent.
Like a solid foundation, what is being described as "solid" is so excellent that it
cannot be made less awesome.

As defined by the Urban Dictionary, this is our goal. Maybe these
are the things that ensure journalists refer to you as a runner rather than
a jogger; hard to say. But solid training guarantees that what you do in
this training cycle provides a platform for continued growth in the next,
whether you hit your target race goal or not. Each decision to follow
through with base building, from your warm-up to doing the prehab,
allows your body to adapt to the ever-changing stresses of running.

Here's where the gel cushioning meets the road and we all realize
that the one true key to better running is **consistency**. In fact, if I could
have chosen my own middle name, it might have been Amanda Consistency Brooks. I'm nothing if not habitual, which at least in running is a
good thing.

Beyond gels and microfibers and the perfect swishing ponytail in
your Instagram photo, it's consistency in training that plays the biggest

role in our success. That consistency isn't just about hitting the miles on a plan, it's doing the prehab from Chapter 4, the dynamic warm-up you'll find here, and showing up for yourself even when a Polar Vortex would make you rather pull the cat fur–laced comforter back over your head.

Quick tip: One of the ways that I like to instill consistency is by working out at the same time every day. Whether you're running, strength training, building that booty, bending like a yogi, or foam rolling because it's a recovery day, showing up for yourself at the same time each day creates a habit, which means you stop relying on motivation and let your subconscious take over.

All day long, we're required to make hundreds of decisions from eating the food we have at home to swinging through the Whole Foods hot bar to answering our boss's untimely request to scheduling that dentist appointment. Each one of these actions sucks away a bit more of our energy and willpower, which means we need our workout to be such a habit that we don't need to consciously choose it; it's simply something we do.

Charles Duhigg explains this very well in his book *The Power of Habit*, which I fully recommend as an audiobook on your next long run. But in the meantime, here's a great quote from it to cement this idea: "Habits are powerful, but delicate. They can emerge outside our consciousness, or can be deliberately designed. They often occur without our permission, but can be reshaped by fiddling with their parts. They shape our lives far more than we realize—they are so strong, in fact, that they cause our brains to cling to them at the exclusion of all else, including common sense."

Your habit might start out as simply setting a time every day where you get into your running gear. Some days, you'll run; some days, you'll strength train; some days, you'll simply sit on the foam roller, pondering life. By showing up at the same time every day, there's a connection created in your brain that, over time, will ensure you no longer need to rely on motivation to get the work done. Because while it's great to feel motivated, it's not reliable.

DYNAMIC WARM-UPS

Out of everything in this book, there are two things I hope you truly take away: you are a runner and you need to do a dynamic warm-up. Realistically, I hope you remember a whole lot of other points, but I'd be satisfied with those two for the time-strapped forgetful among us.

The dynamic warm-up is a sneaky way to insert those glute strength, hip strength, and mobility exercises I've been yammering on about, without adding something to your to-do list. Who says multitasking is always a bad thing?

About ten years ago, it came to me with startling clarity, or through another bout of IT band pain, that I had become exceptionally good at moving my body in a forward motion for hours without stopping. I had become exceptionally bad at doing most other movements. The result was muscle imbalances, pain, time off, and serious frustration. Being a studious type-A runner, I did a complete 180 and decided I would ferret out my weaknesses and beat them into submission with repetition after repetition!

Result: New injuries, burnout, too tired to run.

Although being a full-time athlete would certainly be one route to having plenty of time for all the necessary exercises, warm-ups, cooldowns, massages (yes, you need and deserve those), and variety of runs, it doesn't actually require that much time.

Instead, the goal is to be smarter about our time, finding that happy medium where we maximize enjoyment of the miles with putting in enough work to stay injury-free. No matter how short you are on time, the warm-up is a critical part of your long-term running success. Utilize it to improve not only that run, but all your runs to come. Does that sound too dramatic? Well, then, let me play my favorite card: science.*

---

* Actually, my favorite card is one that my husband gave me back when we were still dating and it's all ooey and gooey with those early lovebird words and inside jokes about our cats, but you can't have that card, so we'll stick with science.

WHY IMPROVE YOUR WARM-UP?

We're all anxious to fit our runs in around that early-morning conference call, the household waking up, or pending weather changes, but neglecting the warm-up is a rookie running mistake. Meaning, obviously, that once you know better from reading this chapter, you shall never again neglect to spend time getting primed to run.

Runners that I coach often seem completely startled to report a few weeks into training that they feel so much better during their runs because of the warm-up I've mandated. I mean, I'm not there and can't give them dirty looks for skipping it, but apparently, they've put their trust in me and are following the plan. What a concept!

During a workout, up to 80 percent of your blood volume is shifted to active muscles. Warming up for twelve to fifteen minutes helps your body transition from rest to action without creating stress on your organs or brain.

In case that still sounded too generic and you still think this a colossal waste of time, let me give you a few reasons that science says it's worth it. Because science never lies, right?*

- Greater efficiency of joints, muscles, tendons, and ligaments
- Greater range of motion
- Increased oxygen availability
- Increased lung capacity
- Release of stored fat for energy
- Creates a routine for mental preparation

If you do not geek out on the science, let's say it a different way:

---

* I will grant you that science can often be found to support nearly any theory. Think you should live on the moon? Here's a study on weightlessness being great for your bones. Nonetheless, how our body functions is a fairly safe bet, so I'm standing by it in this case.

- Allows you to run faster with the same effort
- Ensures you remain injury-free
- Allows you to run farther with the same effort
- Helps you engage more muscles
- Helps prevent muscle imbalances
- Improves postworkout recovery

The kind of warm-up you do doesn't entirely matter, but you might as well get the most out of it with moves that are going to fire up your muscles and prevent injuries. If you begin spending just five to ten minutes before every run doing a few of these moves, you'll find you've incorporated them all throughout the week without any extra gym time.

Since we're all tired of hearing that running is bad for our knees, your assistance in doing these moves to keep yours happy will also be a gift to the entire running community. Supremely helpful if your love language is one of service, but also key if your love language is fueled by endorphins.

How to structure your warm up?

- Incorporate any of the moves listed here.
- Incorporate any of the moves listed in the prehab section.
- Choose a variety to get both strength and mobility in your warm-up.
- Do not hold any static stretches.
- Foam roll before you run, not after.
- Walk for 5 to 10 minutes after these moves.

Each of the following moves is described on one side; please complete repetitions on both sides. You might think that doesn't need to be said, but I have previous angry e-mails to prove otherwise.

Leg Swings

Standing on your right leg, swing your left leg forward with your toes pointed and then back with your foot flexed. Repeat 10 times and then swing your left leg across your body from right to left 10 times.

Lunge Matrix

A personal favorite for working those hips and preventing IT band pain. With your right foot planted and pointing forward, lunge forward, then to the left, then do a front crossover with your left foot pointing forward, then a front crossover with your left foot pointing diagonally to the right. Do 5 reps of each lunge in the same sequence.

Sumo Squat and Raise

With your legs wider than shoulder width and your toes pointed out, lower into a squat, then raise on your toes to come back to standing by engaging those glutes and your core.

Lunge with Rotations

Instead of the lunge matrix, try adding some strength and mobility with this move. With your right foot planted and pointed forward, lunge forward with your left leg and arms straight in front of you. Once in the lunge, rotate your straight arms and torso over your left leg, back to center, and push off to return to standing.

SINGLE-LEG HIP LIFT

Activating our glute medius is difficult with most lunges and squats; this move isolates it for maximum impact. Lying on your back with your knees bent and feet on the floor, pull your right knee in tight to your chest, then using a small movement, press your left heel into the ground to raise your bum.

Once you've finished with all these fantastic moves and your muscles feel like a million bucks, or at least your coffee has started to kick in, it's time to walk. Yes. Walk. Walking moves your body through the full range of motion, starts to raise your heart rate, allows your lungs to open, and adds time on your feet. This isn't a leisurely stroll; it's walking with a purpose for roughly a half mile.

If you have trouble breathing due to asthma or seasonal allergies, this portion of the warm-up can be extremely useful. Try walking for five to seven minutes, then switching to five to ten minutes of run-walk. That period seems to provide time for the lungs to open up and the chest muscles to relax for better breathing, instead of diving right into a more intense steady state of running.

BASE BUILDING

If you were going to create a three-tiered red velvet with buttercream frosting cake, you'd start by selecting a platform that was sturdy, tried, tested, and going to keep everything above from crashing down before you could unveil it at your I-just-PR'ed party.

What, you wouldn't go that big? Why not? I don't bake, but I'm not against finding a good reason to enjoy cake, friends, and celebrating all things running related. Regardless, the tasty metaphor works.

Base building is a bit like us; it's the average, the majority, the vanilla part of training. Or so people would have you believe! But as we know, there's something spectacular about being part of the average crowd, and in this case, it's likely far more interesting than you've been led to believe.

No, you aren't blazing around a track or tackling huge mileage for extra Strava kudos, but you are running for fun, freedom, joy, watch- and worry-free. Which means trying out that new trail run because you have time, joining friends for a no-goals run, or stopping to take 822 running selfies that you can use later.

Embrace the base.*

We try to shorten training schedules or skip right to the goal-pace runs because that's where it feels like progress is made. But speed work without a base is a recipe for red velvet cake in your face. And too many miles without the core foundation is buttercream in your eye, which probably really burns.

One of the biggest things we want to achieve during base building is a more efficient aerobic system. This means that your heart won't need to work as hard at a given pace and will be prepared when you start to add speed or hills, to not overstress your body.

In fact, this goes to the heart of the low-heart-rate training method shared earlier. Although you don't need to stay on that training plan long term, it's a great starting point for every runner, even the experienced ones.

Here's what you should expect from a few months of base-building workouts:

- Flexibility in training to allow for changes due to weather/life
- Improve running economy
- Correct muscle imbalances and minimize injury risk
- Improve breathing while running

---

* It's taking every bit of self-restraint I have not to begin singing, "It's all about that base." If you've gotten the audiobook version of this, then I apologize because I probably didn't hold back.

- Maintain or improve body composition
- Improve mobility and stability
- Psychological benefits
- Improve endurance
- Preventing loss of muscle mass

A good plan is going to incorporate the trifecta of happy healthy running: strength training, cross-training, and easy running.

BASE-BUILDING PLAN GUIDELINES

The first step in any good training plan is to create a foundation to work from. In running, we call that time period base building. The goal is to create a well-rounded body through slowly building the mileage with easy runs and a focus on all the hip, core, and glute strength I've mentioned. When you enter focused race training and may have less time or energy for all the other pieces, your body is primed to handle both the increased miles and intensity from having built a solid foundation.

Base building could be anywhere from six to twelve weeks, depending on your current fitness level or injuries. If you're just starting back up or rehabbing from an injury, it's smarter to take more time on your base to ensure you keep running healthy long term. Rushing the process only to find yourself sidelined is far more frustrating than a few extra weeks of easy running.

A lot of runners choose to utilize winter running for their base building. It's after the fall race season and a good time to focus on all the things listed here, before honing a plan for spring racing.

An example of this base-building schedule is laid out in weeks 1 through 3 of the training plans in Chapter 6. You may start with only two or three runs per week, ensuring you have plenty of time for the other components; longtime runners may be able to handle both strength and a run on the same day, leading to five days of running.

During base building here's what to expect:

- Generally, no speed work
- Easy miles to build your aerobic capacity
- A long run, usually half of your goal distance or less
- Strength training 2 or 3 days per week
- Engraining the need for core-focused workouts
- Cross-training to shore up other muscle weaknesses

Half marathoners might find 8 to 10 miles is their sweet spot for weekend long runs that feel easy and maintain endurance. At the end of this phase, you should be ready to add hills, speed workouts, and tempo runs according to a structured training plan.

The following sections are designed to help lay out how to incorporate core and strength workouts into your base-building routine for maximum benefits. Although these two components are ideal throughout the entirety of your training plan, it's great to take advantage of them early on to create the habits that will keep you doing them once the miles begin to grow.

CROSS-TRAINING

Ugh, I know, I'm about to suggest that you spend time inside a gym* or doing something that is not running. I can't promise that you're going to fall madly in love with it, but I can tell you that focusing on how it will improve your running is helpful in getting you to stick to it.

This is also a chance to find out what other things you might enjoy. It turns out that I think the Pilates Reformer is one of the most amazing

---

* Technically, there's no reason that you can't do many of your core workouts, yoga, body-weight workouts, or cycling outdoors. This is an easy way to start weaving them into your week by combining it with something you already love: sunshine and nature.

medieval torture devices ever. And a few weeks of showing up to classes helped my hips, core, and glutes start to work together better while I run.

Bonus points because working your muscles in different ways means you're less likely to pull a muscle when you take a weird running leap off the curb and you'll improve your stamina through more total body strength.

That's right; while your legs get all the glory, your upper body is actually doing quite a bit of work to help you succeed. The rhythm of your arm swing translates to how quickly you move your legs and powerful arm swings can also help propel you up a hill. A lack of back and core strength could mean you begin to lose form; those muscles fatigue on long runs.

Be open to trying different styles of working out. Enroll in something like ClassPass as an easy way to gain access to a variety of studios and challenge some run friends to meet at a new studio each week. You might be surprised to find yourself enjoying the thumping music and boisterous cheers of a cycle instructor or the calming words of a yogi. Let's look at a few ways these different methods could result in better running.

YOGA

Not only will you be surprised at the strength you can build, but you'll improve your breathing and learn how to mentally work through discomfort, which will benefit you on the run. You can either do an athletic yoga workout or go with a restorative session; in fact, it would be best to do both.

Because running is a constant push, taking a restorative class helps you learn to embrace slowing down. It gives your nervous system a chance to reset, which reduces total body stress for better recovery between workouts and reminds you of the importance of a big deep breath. This idea of slowness is hard for runners, who need to feel the sweat to know it was a workout, which is why I often prescribe this as a recovery day activity. Then, you've mentally set your expectation for why you're taking the class.

PILATES

If you don't know yet that I think working your core is a *key* component of training, you must have skipped some chapters. Pilates is an amazing way to build strength through a complete focus on utilizing the core, which doesn't just mean your abs. These moves are going to strengthen your hips and engage your glutes, which we know is a primary cause of injury in runners.

Mat Pilates is an easy option to do at home, or you can look into a Reformer class. They're a little pricey, but worth going a few times to have an instructor guide you through truly engaging those core muscles.

ROWING

This is another full-body workout that will force you to engage your core and give you some time to work more on that upper body stamina. It's a low-impact option to do HIIT workouts, and using it for intervals can improve the power in your legs for that finish line kick, while remaining lower impact.

CYCLING

Focusing on a cadence of 90 rpm will help you become a better runner by increasing your foot turnover. Ninety rpm mimics the desired 180 steps per minute recommended by most running coaches because it decreases time contacting the ground and often increases your speed without allowing you to overstride.

Head to a spin class, hop on a stationary bike to watch a TV show you wouldn't otherwise, or get some extra motivation by heading outdoors. I don't love biking, but taking the time to seek out routes with incredible views of the mountains certainly helped me enjoy the time and stick with it much longer than if I'd tried to simply head out from home.

SWIMMING

This is another fantastic way to improve lung capacity and create core stability. This low-impact cross-training can be an amazing way to stay on track during many injuries or to get in a cardio workout when you might need a break from intense run training.

In fact, many runners who turn to triathlons find that their run times improved as they started adding these other elements of training. Not only was their body fresher for the runs, but they brought in new skills, strengths, and endurance.

STRENGTH TRAINING

A study in the *Journal of Sports Medicine* showed that strength training can provide up to an 8 percent increase in running economy. That's right; you'll be able to run farther with less effort, and that, my friend, is exactly why we're including strength training as part of our base-building work. We want to make it a natural part of your routine throughout training.

Strength training comes in a lot of forms and there are a lot of opinions on what's best. You've got the CrossFit Endurance crew who say focusing mainly on heavy lifting with only the occasional run is all you need, you've got Orangetheory with high-intensity sprints on the treadmill combined with weights, you've got the crew who thinks running will eat your muscle, and then you have the average runner who doesn't really care about lifting heavy but just wants to see results.

I, my friend, am focused on the last group because that is where I spent many, many, many years. One week, I'd hit the gym a few times; the next week, none at all; and the following week, maybe a core workout outside if I felt so inclined.

Instead, we want to build in that word I so love: consistency. Which means finding a style of training that is most engaging for you. What does that mean? It means there are a lot of ways to get results:

- TRX workouts
- Body-weight-only workouts

- Heavy weights low reps
- Light weights high reps
- Kettlebells
- Dumbbells
- Machines

Our goal is to begin incorporating at least two, if not three, full-body strength-training sessions each week. Here are a few general ideas, to help you test out different types of training and find the one you'll stick with.

HEAVY WEIGHTS

That's right; runners need to utilize a combination of both heavy and lighter-weight strength-training days. Heavy weights help build explosive power and allow us to put on a little more muscle mass, which is important because distance running can eat away at some muscle. These sessions will keep you stronger and move you toward that magazine-promoted word of looking "toned."

Try two sessions per week of just a few exercises, where you go heavy enough to only complete 5 reps:

- Chest press
- Rows
- Shoulder press
- Triceps pull-downs
- Lunges
- Squats
- Deadlifts

LIGHTER WEIGHTS

High-rep weight training can benefit endurance runners because this is, in effect, another form of endurance. It's going to help you continue to pump your arms when tired during the final miles of a race and remain standing tall.

For these movements, I like to sit on a stability ball or stand on one leg, which forces more core engagement. Again, we want to maximize your gym time, so you have less excuse not to get it all done. If you aren't on a stability ball, try standing on one leg, where again you'll be engaging your core and practicing the type of movement that happens in running.

- Shoulder flies
- Alternating bicep curls
- Alternating front shoulder raises
- Alternating triceps press-ups
- Alternating lunge to left, return to standing with shoulder raise
- Triceps dips on a bench
- Push-ups
- Squats with shoulder press and rotation
- Alternating chest flies

BODY-WEIGHT WORKOUTS

Often, the most effective choice for runners is to utilize body weight. We can do it in the park after a run; we can do it in a hotel while traveling or at home without a gym membership. You can absolutely get great results from consistent body-weight workouts, including any of the prehab movements shared earlier.

SINGLE-LEG SQUATS

If you're anything like me, you don't have the range of motion for a pistol squat. We work on that by sitting on a bench with one leg extended. Initially, start by placing the heel of your extended leg on the floor for support, as you engage your glutes to stand or lower yourself.

SIDE PLANK TWIST

With your legs extended with both feet on the floor and your forearms perpendicular to your body on the floor, place your top hand behind your head and then twist your elbow to the ground while thinking about pulling your hips up.

PUSH UP AND BACK

Complete a push-up and then from the top of the push-up, bend your knees and push your body back as if you're going into downward dog but with bent legs. This move should be working your shoulders, not a stretch like downward dog.

REVERSE PLANK

Facing the sky, place your hands below your shoulders with your fingers pointing toward your toes. Engage your core, press your heels and palms into the ground, and raise your hips to form a straight line. Hold up to 30 seconds with all muscles tightly contracted.

SINGLE-LEG REACH

This balance move is fantastic for runner's knee! Standing on your left leg, slowly bend at the waist, reaching your right hand down your shins toward your left foot. Do not try to touch the floor; only go to your range, then return to standing without placing down your right foot.

TRICEPS DIPS

Find a sturdy chair or bench, face away from it, and place your palms on the surface with your fingers pointing toward your bum. Bend your elbows and keep them tight to your sides, as you slowly lower down, then press back up. To increase the intensity, straighten your legs or find a lower platform.

SUPERMAN

Lying on your stomach, contract your core and raise both arms and legs off the floor, hold for 2 counts, and return to the ground.

FULL PLANK

No more holding planks for 2 minutes; it's not working! Instead, you need to implement the focused plank. You should be squeezing every single muscle in your arms, core, glutes, and legs to hold this plank. If you aren't shaking by 15 seconds, you're not squeezing hard enough.

HIP BRIDGE MARCH

Lying on your back, engage your core to raise your hips and, once steady, begin lifting one leg at a time for a march. If your hips are swaying as you march, hold the static bridge until you've developed more core strength.

WHEN YOU'RE READY TO ADD SPEED

Now that you've created a solid foundation through weeks of base building, running hills, core workouts, and strength training, it's finally time to start adding speed. We do those things first to ensure your biomechanics are better, your muscles are stronger to push the pace, and overall your body is ready for the next level of effort. This doesn't mean you go from all easy runs to speed work every other day; there's still a slow and steady process of building your lifetime runner's body.

SPACE OUT SPEED WORKOUTS

Plan your speed workouts at least two to three days before your long run. This provides your legs with enough time to fully recover, ensuring that you're able to complete the long run in good form. You don't need complete rest days after a speed session, but you do need adequate recovery before another hard session or long run.

Starting out, limit yourself to a couple of short sessions each week; then, you can try increasing reps or pace slowly, which is what we'll discuss next! If you're following a training plan, this will likely be done for you. But as a running coach, I've come to realize that even with a plan, many like to improvise. And by improvise, I mean start running everything a lot faster than prescribed because you're excited or start to get nervous about how soon the race is. Stop it.

Your goal is to be the smart runner. The lifelong runner. The crushing course records at age eighty-five runner because you've maintained such great habits learned in this book. Seriously, we're gonna be the biggest group of 80+ Boston Qualifiers ever.

EASE INTO YOUR PACE

Never start your race or run at top speed. Muscles need time to warm up and elongate, which increases blood flow and prevents the dreaded muscle strain. This is where that dynamic warm-up becomes twice as important! If you want more out of your body, then you've got to prep it. Think of it like cooking your weekly frozen pizza. You don't pop it in the cold oven, you turn it on to preheat and, once ready, slide that puppy in, knowing that it will come out with a beautiful crispy crust and bubbling cheese.

Easing into your pace means starting any speed workout with some easy miles. After that, it's about easing in from one workout to the next with steady or slight pace increases. If you've settled on a new race pace goal that's one minute per mile faster, the first workout might include thirty-second bursts at that pace or it might include longer repeats that are only twenty seconds per mile faster than your current pace.

Instead of trying to rush the process, enjoy the feeling of how you react to different paces and get to know what each one feels like. This is going to serve you well on race day.

RUNNING DRILLS

Back to that idea of practicing. Sure, we know *how* to run, but do you run with the most efficient form? Do you run utilizing the most power you can from your push-off? Do you look like the graceful Shalane Flanagan, flowing from step to step?

Of course not; we're not elite runners. Sometimes it looks like we're shuffling by mile 24. But we can improve that and our speed by adding a few drills to our weekly routine. This could turn into its own book, so a few examples:

- High skips
- Quick feet
- Pawing the ground—standing on your right leg, quickly bring your left up in a running motion and practice pawing the ground, catching it with your foot just lightly and quickly bringing your foot up
- Marching in place to practice placing your foot right under your core
- Single-leg step-ups

Plyometric exercises have also proven extremely beneficial to those seeking more speed. That means things like squat jumps, speed skaters, switch lunges, single-leg hops, and yes, even burpees, though I'll deny ever recommending them.

PEAK WEEK

As you've now built the foundation, added hills, added speed, and added mileage, you'll be reaching the precipice of training: peak week. This is the week where every muscle in your body is going to finally be begging you to take one of those rest days you so casually ignored early in training.

According to most studies, we can improve our fitness for four to six months before hitting a temporary plateau, which is why racing can be a valuable part of our running whether we're clock focused or not. By following this method of gradually building, then recovering before the race, you're incrementally taxing your body to create new levels of fitness. Your body will respond better to this training method than pushing yourself to be at peak fitness all the time.

For those who are attempting a new half marathon PR and have been running consistently, peak week could include a run of up to 16 miles. Or for those training to conquer their first marathon it could mean their midweek run is 10 miles and their weekend run is 20-plus miles.

If you're looking at your training plan and terrified of the big week, embrace it. You'll be happier and better off in the long run (literally!) knowing you trained properly. Know that the plan is designed to help you push through the discomfort on race day with the knowledge that you have completed hard runs before. Know that it's designed to give you the power and strength to hit your goal. Know that it's worth it.

WHEN TO PEAK

Old training plans had runners peaking three and four weeks prior to the race, thinking they needed at least that amount of time to recover from the hard effort. However, that mentally destroyed a lot of runners who felt like they were phoning in the last few weeks of training and showed up to the start line feeling sluggish.

Now, the focus is peaking two weeks prior to your race, which means a shortened taper that runners are more likely to fully embrace, plus it's not so much time that you lose the benefits of the gains you made while building up to this tough week.

The goal is to push your body hard, give you a few weeks of recovery, and then let it all loose on race day for a PR, because you've now trained both your body and your mind to go hard. Peak week, however, is *not* the time to try to make up for missed runs or to slack on your nutrition because you're putting in a few more miles and tired.

TAPER THE RIGHT WAY

After surviving peak week, you're finally heading into what is both loved and hated by many runners: taper. It's the time where your mind plays tricks. Was that a niggle or nag in your left knee? Did you power through enough long runs? What do you do with this abundant free time?!

OMG, slow down and let's chat. This is your chance to maximize the benefits of this period of time while your body and mind are still in training mode, rather than revert to maintenance mode.

WHAT TO DO IN TAPER

Taper does not mean plop on the couch and bust out the Cool Ranch Doritos (weren't those the best?!).

Taper does not mean catch up on forty-two overdue work and home projects.

Taper does not mean switch to lots of other workouts because you aren't running.

A two-week taper is a blip in your overall training, which means you've got to use the time wisely. Here's a little breakdown of how that might look.

Day 1—Complete recovery from your longest/hardest run.
Day 2—Get your prerace massage scheduled, at least 6
    days before the race. Enjoy a short run with some
    fartleks.
Day 3—Head out for a medium-distance *easy* run. Do your hip
    strength exercises.

Day 4—Time for another short run with a few speed pickups.
  Do the IT band lunge matrix.

Day 5—Slow it all down with some restorative yoga.

Day 6—Short, easy run and a final test run of what to eat the
  night before your race. More hip exercises.

Day 7—Long run (could be 8 miles for a half marathon or 10 to
  12 for a full).

Day 8—Complete recovery day. Plan out anti-inflammatory
  meals for the week.

Day 9—Enjoy a walk, a hike, yoga flow, or bike ride. Keep it
  easy and fun. Create your race day plan (see Chapter 10).

Day 10—Short run with a few speed pickups. A great day to
  assess your goals and set your mantra.

Day 11—Another good day for restorative yoga and fully planning your race outfit and needs.

Day 12—Short run with a few speed pickups. Focus on a great
  night of sleep.

Day 13—Head to the expo, stay off your feet, hydrate with
  electrolytes, relax!

Day 14—Race day!

This is time to de-stress to the max and take care of your body. But
first, a few other common taper tantrum issues that appear in the mind
and body.

GETTING SICK?

It's very common to develop a cold in the days before a race. Science suggests this is because the body is no longer adrenaline focused pushing you
through weeks of training, and thus the immune system kicks back into
action because it's no longer being suppressed.

Don't fret; nearly all runners find that in these two weeks, if they focus
on recovery, they're ready to rock and roll on race morning. I say that these
colds are the body's way of ensuring we actually follow our taper plan.

EATING TOO MUCH?

Don't stress about calories. Yes, you're running less and technically need less, but hunger pains also decrease after that first week of lower mileage. If you don't go carbo-loading crazy and focus on choosing foods to help your body recover, you'll be just fine.

You want to show up on race day well fueled, not sluggish from restricting your food. Focus on eating when hungry and getting in lots of vegetables for the nutrients and anti-inflammatory recovery properties.

WHAT ABOUT TAPER MADNESS?

As noted, with a short taper, it's less likely you'll find yourself craving more runs, but that doesn't mean you won't have a little taper madness.

Taper madness, coined by longtime runners, refers to the days leading up to the race, when your brain starts to play tricks on you and with longer tapers where you feel completely out of whack due to the massive mileage drop.

Suddenly, things that have never once bothered you in training will hurt. Why are you feeling your big toe in your favorite shoes? Why is your knee tingling? Why did you get a Rudolph-size zit on your nose?!

I can't answer the last one, but I can say that it's all boringly normal. Knowing you aren't alone is the first step in letting go of the stress that's likely creating all your issues. A few other tips that work well:

- Find a mantra, such as "all is well," and use it all week.
- When something hurts, remind yourself that it's likely stress and will be fine on race day (*99 percent of the time, this is true*).
- Get a massage, allow yourself to relax, and treat your body well.

Deep breath; the big day is finally just around the corner. As taper finishes, it's very normal to start feeling nervous and, surprise, that can actually be a really good thing, as we'll discuss in Chapter 10.

DECODING RACE COURSE DESCRIPTIONS

Because I know I'm not alone in finishing a race and wondering whether I missed something on the website, a lifesaving decoder ring for the next race you choose.

Gently rolling hills = lots and lots of hills, which don't feel so gentle after a few hours

Cool temps = it will be frigid at the start line and if you forget throwaway clothes, you won't be able to feel your fingers

Postrace party on the beach = during race sweatfest in the heat

Nice sea breezes = winds to knock you over

Beginner-friendly = we'd like to increase our numbers; please don't be afraid

Scenic = expect no spectators and often feeling like you're running alone

Fast downhill course = your quads will hurt and there's a hill at mile 25

Limited vehicular traffic = ahh, the sweet smell of exhaust

CHAPTER 8

MANAGING RUNGER TO AVOID HANGRY TIMES

Will run for thick-crust Hawaiian pizza! I've now offended you either by putting pineapple on my pizza or by implying that it's okay to run to be able to eat more.

I will not apologize for my pizza love, it's too wonderful and, honestly, I don't understand why you'd fight me over pineapple when so many people put those disgusting black olives on pizza. But I will concede that the longer I've been a runner, the more I think about how eating well helps me feel better and ultimately hit my running goals rather than eating because I've burned calories.*

Runger (please see my Runctionary on page 21, if this word baffles you) is absolutely real. Oddly, the longer you've been running, so is the absence of hunger after a workout. What gives? Why is our body making

---

* Also, I would be a complete liar, if I didn't say it allows me to enjoy treats guilt-free. Because postrun calories don't count, according to 72 percent of doctors that I never polled.

it so difficult to choose cauliflower over Swedish Fish? Why are you ravenous on a rest day and totally uninterested in food on other days?

While training for that first marathon or half marathon, you're likely
increasing your daily activity significantly. Unless you live on a working
farm, in which case, how do you have extra energy for marathon training
and don't you just eat what you grow? Do you grow Swedish Fish? The
body recognizes the extra calorie expenditure and wants to protect you
from famine, as though you were indeed a farmer relying on the land.

Add that our brain runs mostly on glucose, the primary fuel for our
muscles while running. As you might have already guessed, based on the
gel industry, the body burns through tons of glucose to keep our muscles
fueled; when those levels continually drop, we bonk not just from physical exertion, but because our brain is fatigued. Seeking out the quickest
way to level up, our brain leads us to the donut shop instead of the hearty
salad. Unfortunately, that creates a blood sugar spike and, before long,
we're hungry again but likely on the go. We grab a bar or a sandwich
and the volume of carbs again gives us that quick spike and the eventual
drop-off.

Equally important is the emotional side of our brain, which wants to
be rewarded for doing something incredibly hard. Basically, your brain
is a jerk that wants you to not work so hard and to eat really crappy food
to keep it happy. Fat and sugar have been wired into our brain as reward
from an early age, not just through chemistry, but through meaning. We
don't sing "Happy birthday" around a broccoli stalk, we do it with a massive amount of sugar because it's truly a drug to our brain. All that dopamine flooding in cements the connection, and when we're ready to feel
good again, cheap, easy, quick sugar is there to help.

The problem, of course, is that if we allow that to rule too many of
our choices, it undermines our goals.

We gain weight, while doing more than ever. *Confusing beyond belief.*

Our body hurts from the additional inflammation. *Annoying because
we swear, we're foam rolling.*

Moods begin swinging wildly from fatigue and the sugar roller coaster. *Why on Earth are we even training for a stupid marathon?*

This is not a recipe for happy lifelong running. It's leading to the path of one and done, which means we missed out on how this whole journey can change our life for the better. You may be running to lose weight; I did at one point. Or you may simply want to enjoy the miles with less fatigue; I do. Either way, shifting our food focus is going to help with both goals.

Running was the catalyst for my weight loss and has helped me maintain a 35-pound loss for over a decade. But not just because of the calories burned. It made me want to treat my body better, to feel better on my runs, to have more energy and great-looking skin as I age.

I finally gave up the calorie-counting system I'd learned as a chubby teen and started focusing on how to eat more nutritious food. Welcome to my world of freggie counting.* The gold standard for reducing chronic disease and having better health, per a 2017 study published in the *International Journal of Epidemiology*, was ten servings of freggies daily. Less than 13 percent of most adults hit that standard and I was certainly among the masses, but I liked the positive focus of this food goal.

At first, it was a disaster. I couldn't comprehend eating that volume of vegetables. I mean, how do you include veggies at breakfast?! Well, in about a bajillion ways, such as more veggies with your eggs, green smoothies, or my perennial favorite of sneaking zucchini into oatmeal. Slowly, I kept experimenting, gradually adjusting things just as you do with figuring out how to go from running 1 mile to 2 miles.

Along the way, my body started to crave vegetables the way it used to crave cereal. Just kidding; I still love cereal, but I am now the very

---

* In the early days of blogging, I hosted an annual Holiday Challenge to keep us all feeling a little better about our choices. Typing *fruits and veggies* repeatedly became too cumbersome, so *freggies* was born and I still see thousands of those participants saying it, which makes me quite proud. I'll be prouder when more of my Runctionary hits the mainstream.

annoying person on vacation who's whining after a day of grease, "*Oh my gosh, I just want some freaking vegetables*," and makes us walk the extra mile to a restaurant where I can find something beyond iceberg lettuce. In my defense, for that extra mile, you almost always get to split dessert!

Changing the way that you eat doesn't mean ripping apart the kitchen and throwing everything away that's "off plan," after you've had a final tasting, of course. It doesn't mean following a strict diet or cutting out whole food groups. Instead, I hope this helps you come at it from a positive focus on how food makes you feel. Too woo-woo for you to think about how it makes you feel? Okay, let's get concrete:

- Do you feel lethargic after eating?
- Does your skin break out?
- Does your stomach get bloated?
- Do you feel a little queasy?
- Do you end up with runner's trots?
- Do you feel as if you could run for days?
- Do you find yourself hungry again within an hour of eating?
- Does your mood swing high and low? Hello, my sugar-loving friend.

Yes, food can be an emotional topic because it's so closely related to every major event in our lives. But for now, we're pulling that out and focusing on how it quite literally makes your body feel. As a runner, you're in touch with these things, so use it to your advantage.

TIPS FOR MANAGING RUNGER

As a note, I am not a registered dietitian. I am not trying to prescribe a meal plan to you. I am not telling you there is one perfect way to eat. These are the tried-and-true tips that have worked for me, athletes I've coached, and from speaking to many fellow runners who are nutritionists and dietitians.

Remember that you're asking a lot of your body, and to train and perform optimally, you need a sufficient calorie intake. Calorie-cutting during high-volume training leads to illness and injuries, and diminishes your weekly training gains and overall performance. Listen to your hunger cues and do your best to honor those, above all else.

Hunger levels will ebb and flow with the volume and intensity of your training. It's not uncommon to find yourself thoroughly uninterested in food after a track session, but ravenous the following day. On both days, the key is to keep focusing on nutrient-dense foods to ensure your body isn't sending out hunger signals in response to a vitamin deficiency (yes, that totally happens!). Beyond a singular focus on freggies, here are some other tools to manage that "I could eat this entire house" feeling.

REFUEL IMMEDIATELY

This isn't about the magic thirty-minute window that was once the gospel of training recovery, and more recently disproved by studies. The refuel window for maintaining muscle is most important if you've done your run in a fasted state; otherwise, once again, it's about optimal nutrition for recovery.

We're looking at how to refuel in a way that keeps hunger in check—not to avoid a second breakfast, but to avoid the late-night sleeve of Girl Scout Thin Mints. If you've ever tried to take advantage of not feeling hungry, by just waiting 'til later to eat, you know this strategy backfires. Once we get hungry, we're busy or ravenous and eat whatever is handy. We end up eating more, lower-quality calories, than if we'd simply had that planned snack or meal postworkout.

If you're in the not-hungry camp, then welcome to the wide, weird world of green smoothies. One reason they've become so popular is that you can toss in a huge variety of greens, which is a great way to increase your nutrients, aiding your recovery from all those miles. The nutrients can also be more quickly absorbed by the body, since it doesn't need to be broken down via your digestive system. Just be sure your smoothie includes plenty of protein and more greens than fruits, to keep the blood sugar balanced.

A great starter green smoothie: 2 cups spinach, 1/2 banana, 1/2 cup unsweetened vanilla almond milk, 1/2 cup water, 1/2 to 1 scoop protein powder. From there you can get crazy, adding things like shredded broccoli, carrots, Brussels sprouts, and beets. Oh yes, it's true; I do all of that.

If you're in the "I'm so hungry I'll pass out if I don't eat soon" camp, can you cut the hunger with a big glass of water or a scoop of protein powder while you make something hearty, such as eggs, avocado toast, or oatmeal?

PAY ATTENTION TO PROTEIN

In both your postworkout meal and throughout the day, it's important to look at protein and not just carbohydrates. A 2009 study published in *A Current Opinion in Clinical Nutrition and Metabolic Care* stated, "Ingestion of approximately 25–30 g of protein per meal maximally stimulates muscle protein synthesis in both young and older individuals."

After you've had your refuel shake, make the first meal you prepare a bit higher in protein, to help with rebuilding muscles and ensure your body is growing from the workout, not eating your muscle for fuel. This is a large problem for distance runners who start to feel "skinny fat" because they're cutting too many calories for their mileage.

Talking with Dr. Bob Seebohar, a sport dietitian for the US Olympic Committee, gave me a new level of appreciation for focusing on more protein than carbs with every meal. It prevents that roller coaster of insulin that leads to ongoing hunger surges throughout the day. Plus, the increased protein to balance out those carbs actually allows the body to use more fat than carbs for fuel while at rest and during the run. This is great for controlling blood sugar, reducing body fat, and ensuring you don't need as many gels during the workout.

Don't get fixated on macros; instead, practice making protein a consistent part of your meal, and you'll be spreading it evenly throughout the day for optimal absorption and use by your body.

SPEND LESS TIME THINKING ABOUT FATS

Fats are so important in the diet, especially for athletes. If you've started to focus on consistently adding protein, you may not need to think much more about fat. That tablespoon of nut butter for a snack is a perfect protein and fat combo; the stir-fry with coconut oil has you covered; and the turkey jerky on the trail is nailing it, too.

If you're still running low, then try adding a tablespoon of coconut oil to your smoothies or enjoying more avocado on your salad or Instagram-worthy avocado toast with salmon for more protein.

A lack of fat is one of the reasons you might find yourself craving nut butters! They provide more than just fats, they also hit on other key runner nutrients and, let's be honest, they simply bring a smile to the face and warm the heart. If you are someone who eats it straight from the jar, like moi, make sure you know a serving size, otherwise this perfectly balanced treat could be undoing your progress, too, with excess calories.

CARBS ARE YOUR FRIEND

Avoiding carbs is like trying to run without Body Glide. You can do it, but it won't feel that great. Every sports nutritionist is going to encourage complex carbohydrates, from vegetables and whole grains (sweet potatoes, squash, quinoa, oats), as part of your diet.

These foods provide both energy and important vitamins and minerals. Simple carbohydrates, coming from refined grains and processed foods (think: crackers, cookies, chips, candy, soda, etc.) can certainly be enjoyed occasionally or even as fuel during a run, but they aren't optimal to keep the body feeling strong throughout training.

It's easy to feel you've earned the cronut, everything bagel, or vegan gluten-free vanilla cupcake, but if marathon-size hunger is something you're experiencing, it's time to shut down the "I deserve it" mind-set. Finding a way to break that connection of rewarding yourself with sugary foods isn't always easy, but once you've started to add the protein and the fats, you will find your body craves sugar less. Then, it's about setting yourself up for success. Like asking the run group to stop finishing that 3-mile run at the donut shop!

Hopefully, by now you're starting to see the connection between energy swings, hunger levels, and those high-carb meals. This doesn't mean I'm pushing you to go low carb, just more carbohydrate selective. Later in this chapter, we'll dive into the high-carb vs. low-carb debate, but first, let's finish these tips to manage marathon training hunger.

SLEEP LIKE IT'S A SECOND WORKOUT

Did you know that you may need up to nine or even ten hours of sleep for your body to fully recharge?! Our elite idols often get twelve hours of sleep by napping during the day. In fact, a sleep study at Stanford noted that athletes who "increased their sleep time ran faster sprints and hit more accurate tennis shots than they did while getting their usual amount of sleep."

Your body is doing so much while you sleep that I think we need to start considering it a workout.*

- Sleep is when your body produces **human growth hormone** (HGH), which stimulates muscle growth and repair.
- In sleep deprivation, you produce less HGH and your muscles pay the price with slower progress.
- Sleep is when your body synthesizes protein, creates new cells, repairs tissue, and **boosts your immune system**.

---

* Sleep is possibly my second favorite thing next to running and if I now realize that it's also a workout, whoa, multitasking taken to the next level. Second book idea: "Sleeping My Way to Better Running" by testing out lots of beds, blankets, and sleeping positions. Brilliant.

- Sleep deprivation combined with workout exertion is when you're more likely to get sick and, of course, all your runs feel crummy.
- In sleep deprivation, we feel hungrier. Add that to distance running and it explains the never-ending runger.
- In sleep deprivation, the body is less effective at converting carbs to glycogen—hello, **hitting the wall**.

How much sleep do runners need? A good rule is to add one minute per mile you're running per week. This comes as a shock to many runners, but it makes sense. If you ask more of your body, you need to give it more time to recover.

Example: If you need 8 hours of sleep to feel well rested when you aren't training and are now doing 40 miles a week, aim for 8 hours 40 minutes most nights.

NEVER SKIMP ON ELECTROLYTES

Electrolytes are an important component of sports nutrition and one of the easiest things to quickly resolve when the body feels out of whack. Following are the five main electrolytes and some of the most common issues created from being low in them (not just for runners, but anyone with an imbalance):

- Calcium: helps with muscle contractions, maintaining bone health
- Potassium: keeps blood pressure stable
- Magnesium: aids muscle contractions, nerve functions, bone density, anxiety reduction
- Sodium: maintains fluid balance, nerve signaling
- Chloride: maintains fluid balance

First, you can see it's about more than sodium, so your salty food isn't enough to keep you balanced. Although it might taste good, we need to keep ingested sodium generally balanced for total heart health. Second, some of the symptoms you might have been attributing to overtraining or just a bad day, a quick sports drink or tablet might resolve. It's no wonder Gatorade convinced everyone to grab a neon-colored beverage and guzzle it; the concept works. Now, luckily, there are lower-sugar, less-industrial-ingredient options available.

A few additional reasons for runners to pay attention to electrolytes:

1. Balanced electrolytes prevent fatigue, lightheadedness, and decreased performance.
2. Salt tablets (or salty foods) only provide two of the five electrolytes that you need to stay balanced.
3. You can't replace what you've lost all at once, which is why it's best to consume electrolytes during and postexercise.
4. Runner's trots are also thought to be caused by an imbalance of electrolytes (don't overdo the sugary sports drinks; that could cause issues, too).
5. Muscle cramps while running are one way your body tries to alert you to an electrolyte-balance issue.

Because you're staying well hydrated, *right?* and you're also sweating copious amounts, thanks to running, it's easy to flush your body of electrolytes. Which is why you need to pay attention to electrolyte replacement. Whether you opt for a homemade version like Shalane Flanagan's blackstrap molasses and coconut water, or opt for the lazier version of premade, as I do, you're going to reap the benefits.

While marathon training in Miami, I needed to take a SaltStick tablet prerun and then sip electrolytes throughout the run to have any chance at staying on top of my electrolyte balance and hydration. Conversely, in Denver, as long as I'm drinking electrolytes at some point during the day, I feel pretty good.

You can find electrolytes in whole foods, such as pickle juice, bananas, and coconut water, if you prefer to go that route. Just make sure you're getting in enough, at the right times.

RUNNING WITH WHOLE FOODS

Another way to manage hunger is fueling enough during long runs. This goes back to that whole-brain glucose thing. If your brain isn't depleted, it's less likely to force you to stop, and if your stomach isn't growling, you're less likely to feel as if you might pass out without food.

This doesn't mean you need to take in the number of calories you're burning every hour. More and more that old mind-set is being left behind as people's stomachs and waistlines revolted. One of the most fascinating things I've noticed over the years is that road runners feel very tied to the quick hit of gels, whereas trail runners are all about whole food sources. There's certainly a difference in intensity, which means road runners can't handle the same volume of food, but there's a lot we can learn and test on road runs to find alternative fuels.

Consuming enough calories before you head out to run, and then postrun, is your opportunity to load up on whole foods as a primary fuel source, lessening the need for fueling during the run. For many runners, those two pieces can carry them through 10- to 13-mile runs without extra gels, blocks, and so on.

HOW MANY CALORIES DO YOU NEED DURING A RUN?

It's time to stop thinking in calories and focus on the kind of fuel you're burning and how you handle sustained energy. That sounded a little clinical, so let's break down the great conversations about fueling I've been having lately with sports scientists and nutritionists.

1. Standard recommendations are based on male runners and often report anywhere from 120 to 300 calories per hour. Women, however, generally burn far fewer calories than men, and depending on their efficiency, *need* far fewer than that.
2. Work on building your aerobic base first, as described in base building (page 143). This ensures you're burning more fat on

those long runs and will need less quick fuel to sustain your energy.

3. Shorter workouts usually will not require any food during the session. Short could mean up to 13 miles, depending upon your exercise intensity and, again, heart rate. Most runners can do up to 7 to 9 miles without consuming calories during the run. This is where electrolyte drinks become even more helpful, alongside those pre- and postworkout meals.

4. High-intensity runs, such as intervals, tempos, or even long runs are best done with a solid amount of prefueling. In these cases, a fasted run is more likely to result in hindered performance or bonking.

5. Test for yourself: Do you feel grumpy late in your run? Probably out of carbohydrates. Do you get a lot of stomach issues? Probably too many sugars or hard-to-digest foods. Do you finish a run without fuel feeling as good as when you started? Then you're on to something, so don't let the idea that you *must* fuel change your plan.

6. Which is all to say, stop paying attention to the amount you're burning as a guide to what you take in on the run. Instead, pay attention to your energy levels.

The one caveat here is race day. On race day, your intensity level will go up, crossing the threshold from mostly fat to mostly carbs needed for fuel. The body is going to be looking for quick carbs to create quick energy. Although most people can still use far less than the recommended one gel per thirty to forty-five minutes, you may find that half a gel or a couple of Clif Bloks every 4 to 5 miles are just enough to keep your energy steady.

Gels became popular because of this need for a quick energy source when your body is using more carbohydrates for fuel. Unfortunately, they have to go through your gut before entering the bloodstream to provide energy to your muscles. That's where many runners experience stomach problems, not to mention the roller coaster of sugar spikes and drop-offs' messing with energy.

Now, the number of natural and whole food energy options has exploded into a whole new industry, giving us plenty of variety to test during training runs. Although the ideal scenario is to use whole foods, that isn't always practical or digestible.

TIPS FOR FUELING LONG RUNS WITH WHOLE FOODS

A few important notes from athletes who have transitioned to natural running fuel, a.k.a. whole foods:

- Eat more frequently, but less volume (every 30 to 45 minutes).
- Consider a mix of whole foods and processed carbs for endurance events, to ensure adequate calories and quick carbs to the muscles.
- Always test on training runs before race day.
- Aim for low-fiber whole foods.
- Consider using more homemade gels and drinks during higher intensity.
- Start with carbs before the race (e.g., toast, banana, oatmeal).

QUICK WHOLE FOOD IDEAS

There are a lot of options; I'm going to range from the easiest for most people to stomach to those that the ultra-athletes found helpful.

- Bananas
- Dried pineapple (helpful for digestion)
- Dates with coconut oil (Larabar is more expensive, but faster)
- Dried apricots (good source of iron) plus a couple of almonds
- Packet of nut butter
- Trail mix

- Squeeze packet of fruits/veggies
- Boiled eggs (a favorite of Ironman training folks)
- Homemade energy balls of nuts, seeds, etc.
- Boiled potatoes with Himalayan pink sea salt (just wrap in foil and go)

The downside to whole foods, which must be addressed, is that if you're trying to replicate the carbohydrates in a gel, you need a greater volume and your body is going to need to digest these whole foods to extract the energy. As always, you need to test out different options during training to see whether your body handles the volume of food without issue and provides you with the needed energy during long runs.

Also, some gels, gummies, and energy foods on the market have proven easier for many runners. A few notable ones: Honey Stinger Waffles or Gels, Clif Bloks, Jelly Belly Sport Beans, Huma Gels, and Tailwind Endurance Drink.

Although much of the original science recommended taking one gel packet per thirty to forty-five minutes of running, I've never found that my body needed that volume of sugar during a marathon. It turns out that this intuitive style of eating and fueling was right all along, per my notes earlier from Dr. Bob Seebohar. If you feel that you've been forcing yourself to down more gels than feels good or simply eating more on the run than you'd like, don't be afraid to cut it down. Just continue to pay attention to those high-quality pre- and postrun meals.

Now that we've addressed our runger, here are a few more common questions about fueling.

WHAT ABOUT A PREWORKOUT SUPPLEMENT?

Since you now know that you don't have to eat before an easier session, or if you do eat, you might not need calories on the go, where does a preworkout supplement fit into the mix?

Again, each runner is different and you need to know how your body reacts to stimulants. As one of the world's few non-coffee drinkers, I generally avoid caffeine except on specific long or intense training runs and then on race day. It becomes like rocket fuel for my body and I love that added boost. As it peaks around forty-five minutes after ingestion, it's good to use right before you start, and then take something with caffeine throughout the long run to maintain that stable energy.

If you're a consistent coffee drinker, you might just be blown away by what happens if you cut it out for three weeks prior to the race and then enjoy it on race morning. It could help you sleep more during taper, too, which is a double win. Crankiness is a known side effect of taper, so you can blame that for the withdrawal symptoms.

Beyond coffee, there are a slew of preworkout supplements on the market. And studies seem to indicate it might be worth your time to test them out on hard workout days or for long runs. As stated by sports nutritionist Drew Price to *Men's Health*, "Caffeine [or its herbal counterparts] reduces levels of perceived effort so you can train harder. It improves your body's ability to use fatty acids for energy, conserving carb stores and delaying fatigue."

All of that sounds like a win, win, win. Yet, still, I caution against using them for every single run because I believe that, just as you soon need that second and third cup of coffee to feel awake, you'll also adapt to those energy boosters. Beyond that, on easy days, you want to be entirely in touch with how your body feels and not pushing too hard because of something external dampening those signals.

WHAT ABOUT LOW-CARB RUNNING?

Keto is like pop star tabloid magazine cover everyone seems to be drooling over these days. A few years ago, we called this Atkins. A few years before that, it was likely some other diet with the same concept of focusing on more fats in your diet, restricting carbs, and teaching your body to function on fat.*

---

* Have you ever seen the *Vogue* wine diet? It basically prescribes a glass of wine with each meal as part of your weight-loss plan; yup, even with breakfast. Ahh, the good old days when people weren't afraid of carbs and had very little use for nutrition.

Although teaching your body to utilize more fat for fuel is a critical component of improving endurance, it doesn't mean that your body no longer needs carbohydrates. At all times, your body is burning *both* fat and carbohydrates for energy; however, you can train it to rely on more fats, as discussed.

With studies now showing the long-term health risks associated with a Keto diet, I personally cannot endorse it. That does not mean, however, that it doesn't work for some people. Cayenne pepper lemonade and cabbage soup diets worked for some folks, too.

Bio-individuality is a concept that I believe applies to both our running and our nutrition. We all have similarities, but we're each an experiment of one and need to be willing to open our mind to lots of ideas to find the thing that works best for us. And when that thing is no longer working because our lives have changed, hormones have shifted, or preferences altered, then we need to ensure we aren't so tied to a label that we stick to something no longer beneficial.

What do I mean by that? Vegan. There's a very strict label and one that probably brings up a lot of connotations based on whether you use it or are heartily against it. Either way, it's a plant-based diet that can ensure you get a boatload of nutrients and has a great deal of science behind its heart health benefits.

Unfortunately, being tied to the label for some runners meant they stuck with veganism for years while feeling run down and fatigued, and battling constant injuries. For those runners, a blood test often convinced them that adding a little animal-based protein each week might improve their results . . . and it did.

You can eat however you choose! Just ensure you're choosing what feels best, not being driven by a label.

HOW DO HIGH-FAT DIETS WORK?

Based on the ketosis model to kick your fat burners into gear, you need to eat less than 50 grams of carbohydrates per day and never exceed 75 percent of aerobic capacity. In a study of elite endurance athletes, they were required to restrict carbs for at least six months to see enough changes for a worthwhile test.

Following a high-fat diet for six months while training and maintaining your lifestyle isn't easy. That means bye-bye to breads and nearly all starchy vegetables, very few fruits, and of course, no sugary treats or gels fueling those runs. Meanwhile, you still need to get in enough nutrients to help your body recover from the stress of training.

To truly follow this diet, you can't have some high-carb days and some low-carb days; it's all in or nothing. Why, then, are you hearing more about it from many endurance athletes? These are the benefits they believe outweigh the health implications:

- Body uses fat for fuel, no need for all those carbs while training and racing.
- Weight remains stable.
- Hunger decreases.
- Cancer cells are starved without the sugars and carbs.
- Energy increases.
- It keeps blood sugar stable, and increases metabolism.
- Endurance increases, removing the dreaded bonk.
- It improves recovery and reduces inflammation.

Although I'm not so concerned about eliminating gels or junky carbs, let's consider the idea that we're restricting vegetables and fruits. Nutrients. Restricting nutrients, while asking your body to day in and day out perform optimally for you, seems like a really weird tradeoff for a couple of pounds. Especially, when you could look at creating meals with equal amounts of carbs and protein to create the balanced blood sugar effect, instead of cutting out whole categories of food.

I still remember running alongside Olympian Deena Kastor, having a conversation about fueling, when she said, "Fats burn in a carbohydrate flame." She was simplifying the science that states fat can only be oxidized for fuel when carbohydrates are present, and for runners that means restricting one huge source of fuel is also limiting our ability to capitalize on fat.

WHAT ABOUT CARB LOADING?

If I'm not a fan of restricting carbohydrates, does this mean I'm a super-fan of carb loading? Nope.

It's another extreme and usually botched by most runners.

For years, we've heard of nothing but the glorious days of carb loading for marathon day, which means mounds of bagels, beautiful plates of pasta, and let's not pretend we shun the cookies. Not anymore.

After my first few races, I realized that, for the most part, carb loading before a race left me feeling *groggy, bloated, and lethargic.* It turns out that this is a rather common feeling among many runners, but they don't realize that the cause is the carb-loading myth, which we've passed around from runner to runner. Not to mention that one plate of pasta isn't carb-loading.

If you're new to the concept, *carbohydrate loading* is a strategy proclaimed to maximize muscle glycogen (carbohydrate) stores prior to endurance competition. Athletes believe that by loading the muscles with glycogen, they can prevent hitting the wall and run at their desired pace for a longer duration.

Done correctly, carbohydrate loading has the potential to improve performance by 2 to 3 percent. For a two-hour half marathon, that is an improvement of **roughly 2.4 to 3.6 minutes** or nearly 7 minutes for a four-hour marathon. Ahhh, now we see why people are so excited to try this, besides the extra everything bagel at breakfast.

A two- to three-minute change in time is the difference between making that sub-two-hour half marathon goal and being just over it once again. Unfortunately, most of us don't fully understand what carbohydrate loading is and our well-intentioned pasta dinner leaves us with a 2 percent decrease in performance instead!

In fact, you know who carbohydrate loading will only work for . . . all those folks following a ketogenic diet! What?! The carbohydrate-loading protocol was developed by the military and required soldiers to be carb depleted (read: totally exhausted) for over a month, then they were given a diet of 70 percent carbohydrates prior to a big mission and miraculously had a massive influx of energy. Just like when kids go haywire after looting their Halloween candy.

For you to get the same benefit, you're going to have to suffer through some carb depletion.

Here is the process as described in *The Complete Nutrition Guide for Triathletes*.

1. Seven days prior to the event, do a long or strenuous workout, which will deplete your body of glucose.
2. For the next 3 days, maintain a lower carb diet of 35 to 50% of total calories.
3. For the final 2 days prior to the race, switch to 75% of calories from carbohydrates, while dramatically decreasing overall work volume (the other 25% is largely protein).

A few key points from this process:

- Loading isn't a 2-week feast, it is a couple of days of an increase.
- Loading doesn't mean cookies and cakes; it's more fruits, whole grains, and potatoes.
- Loading is important the morning of your race.
- This is not a long-term style of eating, but a short burst before the race of depletion and reloading.

In either the carb-loading scenario or ketosis, you're putting your body through extremes, and we've already decided that around here our goal is to enjoy the middle. You can make carbohydrates a consistent part of your meals, skip worrying about any massive carb-loading phase, and enjoy both great runs and great health.

The "perfect diet" is one that works for your body and, indeed, it may not be what works for your significant other, your running buddy, or your annoying cubicle mate. For example, Greek yogurt is a fantastic snack, unless like me you've figured out dairy is an issue and then, boom, you've created inflammation that sinks your running.

You'll notice we haven't talked about calories yet, and that's because this isn't a weight-loss book. Our goal is finding the foods and style of eating that you cannot only maintain to run your best, but actually enjoy!*

Having said that, let's circle back to this idea of eating ten servings of freggies a day. Kids need to be exposed to a new food up to twenty times before they accept it, so plan on experimenting with yourself to find the foods that you enjoy and your taste buds will get on board.

Since I know you're every bit the busy runner that I am, I'm going to share some of my very lazy, very easy ways to sneak more veggies into your life.

1. Shredded carrots blend right into oatmeal and bulk it up.
2. Shredded zucchini works in breads and muffins.
3. Cauliflower puree can replace half (or all) of your mashed potatoes for the same flavor.**
4. Smoothies make almost any vegetable disappear when blended with a little fruit and vanilla almond milk.
5. Chili need not only contain beans, meat, and tomatoes; it's the perfect place for a variety of diced peppers, onions, carrots—all making it more colorful and appetizing.
6. Mushrooms are easily hidden in ground turkey for tacos.

---

* That's right, enjoy your food. I'm all for my postrun green smoothie, but that doesn't preclude my daily dark chocolate or my Friday night slice of pizza to connect with my husband.
** Don't talk to me about cauliflower pizza crust, though; you've taken things too far.

7. Wilted spinach can hide out under the cheese on your homemade pizzas.

8. Opt for homemade salsas to ensure there are whole onions, tomatoes, and peppers being piled on to any Mexican feast.

9. Spaghetti squash! Add some meatballs and your sauce; the family might notice the texture, but the taste will convince them to keep eating.

10. Sweet potatoes, mushrooms, summer squash, zucchini, and almost any other veggie, when finely diced, are easy to slip into a breakfast or dinner scramble.

You might have also guessed that the bonus to eating these foods is you increase the volume of your meals and eat more fiber, without increasing your total calories. Ta-da, another winning solution to battling runger.

Don't be afraid to continue trying new things to find out what makes you feel the best. There's going to be a balance that allows you to feel energized from runs and maintain your health, your weight, and your sanity. No extremes here in the middle; we're just living our best lives.

RUNNER PET PEEVES

Nothing ruins a great run faster than someone messing with your Zen.

Why are you staring at me as you drive? Do you wish you were out running, too?

Why do you get on the treadmill next to me when there are 22 open machines? Now, we have to race.

Why are you asking if I won? Don't you think I'd tell you that first . . . and do you really think I'd win?

Why are you telling me why you don't run? That's a personal choice.

Why is every injury because I'm a runner? Maybe I'm clumsy.

Why are you honking at me? Do you think I'll stop running and come make out with you?

Why do they keep changing running shoes that are absolutely perfect? Do they want me to buy a new brand?

CHAPTER 9

UNDERSTANDING THE FINAL 10%

It's the final countdown, nah, nah, nahhhhhhhhhhh. This song runs through my head at every start line; though I may not have heard it for years and know literally that one refrain, it sets off the Go time bell in my mind. It feels appropriate as right now I want to chat about the last 10 percent of training, which too often gets at least 50 percent of our focus. The extras. The gear. The supplements.

We love it. It's fun. It's motivating. It's colorful (or all black for my NYC friends). But at the end of the day, these tools are just 10 percent of the equation when it comes to performance. Those of us who have been running long enough to remember rolling the top down on our mesh shorts, wearing a white cotton T-shirt purchased from Goodwill "because it was just going to get sweaty," will tell you those things didn't hinder our races.

Life is certainly more comfortable and less chafy with Dri-FIT, wicking, superpolyfragilistcal fibers, but not necessarily faster. Unlike triathlon, where the tiniest change in weight on your bike or shaving your legs at the last minute before a race can give you time benefits, in running, our gear is usually more about comfort.

A BASIC RUNNER'S CLOSET

After seventeen years running and twelve years writing about running, it's fair to say my closet is no longer basic. It's often bursting at the seams with new gadgets, gizmos, fibers, and shoes I've been allowed to test. The things that don't stick for me are donated on a quarterly basis.

But I will say that I use the same few pieces over and over again. If I were back in my early years of running, as a broke college kid, I'd be judicious with my dollars and focus on the gear I now believe provides the most value.

I HAVE ENOUGH SHOES . . . SAID NO RUNNER EVER

I know the second I say high-quality running shoes, you are going to skim right over this section; please don't! It's not always the duh you think. For the first two years, I ran in whatever shoes I happened to find on sale at the big department stores (as noted cheap college kid) because I didn't realize they are actually *different* than what is sold by a running store.

Notice also that I said shoes. I'm a firm believer in having at least two pairs for rotation. Not only because it makes us happy, but for some practical reasons as well.

The *Scandinavian Journal of Medicine and Science in Sports* showed that runners rotating at least two models were 39 percent less likely to get injured. There, now you have just cause to show anyone questioning your spending, you are saving on future medical bills.

A few key reasons could explain their findings:

1. Shoes have bounce. You know each brand loves to talk about its latest and greatest foam or cushion, but did you know that a shoe can take up to 24 hours to bounce back from a run?

2. Our body loves to adapt to stimuli, and running in the same shoe over and over means we start to rely on the support or the feel, which allows muscles to become weak or imbalanced.

3. Different shoes can serve different needs from long runs to speed workouts to trail runs. The form, weight, and tread you look for may change.

HOW DO YOU DECIDE ON THE RIGHT SHOE?

For most clothing, you traipse into a poorly lit changing room. You uncomfortably strip down and then pull on the new gear, wondering why you appear to have a yellow tint to your skin. You turn around a few times and a decision is made. This is *not* how you buy running shoes.

Head to your local running store and embrace its expertise in shoes. Put on a variety of shoes, walk out the front door, and run around the block! That's right, the staff will let you actually run in them. None of this couple-of-steps-forward-and-back; how is that possibly going to tell you what they feel like running?

Don't buy a specific shoe simply because it's recommended. If it doesn't feel good on your foot, that matters!* Many places will also let you return a pair after you've taken them for a run and realized they simply were not the right choice for you. But your running store can also show you different ways to lace your shoes, which could mean a pair you've not been wearing is suddenly the right fit again.

BEAT BACK THE CHAFE

Whether you opt for a gel or a stick or a lotion, an antichafe solution is worth every single penny. Even when you've got on gear that wicks away sweat, it's common to find that a random seam is rubbing you the wrong way.

---

* Also, if they have you run on a treadmill and then recommend a stability shoe, please beware. Looking only at your ankle is not diagnosing if the actual issue is your weak hips. Wearing a stability shoe could mask that issue for a bit, but ultimately make things worse. Strength first, then support.

The repeated motion of running makes it easy to find hot spots or points of friction, which lead to that painful red skin irritation, which you sometimes notice on the run, but most often notice when the shower hits it and you scream bloody murder.

Gents, I'm going to save you some long-term trouble as well. Buy nipple guards or invest in a large package of Band-Aids. Ladies don't have the same issue because our sports bras keep shirts from moving back and forth across that area, which doesn't just chafe but with continued friction will bleed. Yikes! This is the excuse many of my male friends make for why they must run shirt-free, but I think we all know they really just want the extra vitamin D.

Don't Chintz on Your Socks

Fifteen dollars for a freaking pair of socks?! You've got to be joshing me, my mom said in much less kid-friendly language. We used to buy a twelve-pack of cotton socks for less. Yet, that was what I wanted as an adult for Christmas, socks, my once dreaded childhood present.

We runners are always thinking about what we put on our feet. I mean, there are pink shoes with cord laces and blue shoes with a 10-foot cushioned sole and superspeedy-looking yellow shoes meant to mimic our bare feet. Beyond that, we don't give our feet the attention they deserve for all the pounding they take, until something hurts.

Skip the cotton; be okay with spending a bit more for the right technical material and fit. A great pair of socks will eliminate a few major issues:

- Friction (blisters and black toenails)
- Heat (discomfort, swelling, blisters)
- Moisture (blisters, swamp foot bacteria, feeling cold)
- Rubbing (blisters, raw skin)

Even one of those could put you off running for a couple of days or a week because you can't pull on a shoe without severe pain. Which means a major interruption to your training and your goals.

They See Me Rollin'

Unlike the wicked stepmother that you will never grow to love, the foam roller is an evil little tool that you'll find yourself missing when you travel. I know that sounds like a big promise, but give it time. Although it can feel like a massage, we're not just working with our muscles; instead, we're focused on the fascia.

Fascia is connective tissue that provides stability and connection for everything in our body. A good way to think of it is that your skin is like the outer layer of an orange and the fascia is that white layer that connects everything and gives it structure!

When our fascia gets tight or twisted, through stress, training, overuse, underuse, movement imbalances, and injuries, we develop what are referred to as muscle adhesions . . . or those "knots" and trigger points everyone tells you to roll on.

We want to break up those adhesions to prevent any additional imbalances from muscles' being pulled too tightly or restricting blood flow.

So, You Had a Bad Date

Are the puns working for anyone besides me? Allotting a portion of your gear spending to groceries sounds like a bizarre one, but honestly, I'd rather see you paying for prechopped veggies to get in those quality meals, than paying for gels. By now, we've all heard that abs are made in the kitchen, which is great, but more important for us is that recovery, energy, endurance, and mood boosting starts here, too.

Our runs might be how we release the stress of the day, but without the right fuel, we're going to keep having more bad runs and achy knees, which I just can't explain one more time to a nonrunner. A few ways to save and splurge for staying on track in the kitchen:

- Enroll in a local CSA.
- Make the farmers' market part of your post–long run routine.
- Buy prechopped veggies.
- Buy higher-quality cuts of meat to reduce antibiotics and hormones.

- Embrace slow cooker and batch cooking to have leftovers.
- Try a meal kit delivery service.
- Opt for homemade pizza.

Our goal isn't to eliminate anything deemed not perfectly healthy. We just want to find ways to make it easier to enjoy what you've got at home than the 500-calorie Starbucks Unicorn drink and 350-calorie muffin to go with it.

WHEN IT'S COLD AS . . .

Winter base layers may not seem basic, but one of the lessons we quickly learn is that having the right gear makes winter running far more enjoyable. Through those college training years, I wore cotton long-sleeved shirts and other assorted nontechnical fabrics, which left me cold to the bone as my sweat was absorbed and then simply sat on my skin in the 30-degree temperatures.

As a smarter runner, I invested in a pair of fleece-lined running tights, a base layer running shirt, and a warm long-sleeved running top, all to go with my Drift beanie and gloves. Suddenly, winter wasn't so scary and I found myself enjoying the quiet solitude of the mornings or the crispness of the air.

These items should last you for many, many runs and winters, so consider them a long-term investment. Another reason to run for a lifetime and not a race.

KEEP TRACK OF YOUR DIGITS

As noted in base layers, I swear by wicking gloves. Oftentimes, I can head out in shorts, but still need gloves for the first few miles to make the chill bearable. This is because your body is pushing all the blood through your core to keep you warm and move your legs, so it's not worried about those fingers, which are just hanging out doing nothing important.

Comfort might not be the first thing to come to mind when you think of running, but why not make choices to keep you from making excuses. Unless that excuse is buying new running gear, and then I like it.

WHAT TIME IS IT?

A basic GPS watch is way down the list because you probably now carry a phone while running. There are a ton of free smartphone apps that will track your route and pace, using a GPS signal, meaning you don't need Wi-Fi or cell service. I, however, really like to quickly check my watch and utilize the wrist-based heart rate monitoring, which is where you might say, "That's why I got an Apple watch," and aren't you fancy.

Most GPS brands offer an entry-level model with limited features, and that's all you need to get started. In fact, it's all most of us need for the majority of our running: GPS tracking, lap splits, maybe a timer. This is just a tool to make things a little bit easier for you, not to make you a better runner, so don't feel that you have to splurge on the most expensive model to be a real runner.

THE FUTURE'S SO BRIGHT

Did you know wearing the wrong sunglasses could actually result in a bad run? I am a little ashamed to admit this, but I spent a lot of years running without sunglasses because they bothered me and I didn't know what I was missing.

If you, like me, couldn't understand why you'd need to purchase an expensive pair of sunglasses, *please* read this:

- Squinting creates stress.
- Stress tells your brain you're doing something hard.
- Thinking that running is hard tells your brain it's hard.
- Eye strain leads to fatigue and headaches.
- Lack of eye protection isn't cool when running on roads with things flying about.
- UV exposure can lead to cataracts and other issues.
- All that squinting adds to the lines around your eyes.

What struck this very cheap runner the most was how buying low-quality sunglasses can distort your vision, which leads to headaches, and of course your brain working harder to try to fix the image (less energy for your run). This is one instance in the Basic Closet to go for the top tier and then take very good care of them so they last for years.

KEEPING MORE MOOLA IN THE BANK

Since I do have twenty-two pairs of running shoes and a closet that could double as a running store, it might come as a surprise to you that I'm superthrifty and a minimalist in most ways! If it weren't for the perks of my job, I'd probably wear four pairs of shoes and the same five pairs of shorts and shirts, every single week.

Back in the old days when I started running as a broke college kid and then a broke just graduated twenty-something, I knew the benefit of gear, but still had to do it without breaking the bank. Here are some of my favorite money-saving tips:

- Shop at places like TJ Maxx or Marshalls—I bought all my first winter gear there.
- Shop online with Poshmark for gently used gear.
- Follow runners like RunToTheFinish on Instagram for giveaways.
- Watch your local running stores for events; they often do up to 20% discounts on those nights, which is an opportune time to buy shoes.
- Buy your current shoe model when the new one is released; it should be on clearance.
- Remember that newer brands and less expensive brands can still make great gear; don't let labels drive your buying decisions.
- Register for races as soon as they finish. This will often be their cheapest price for the following year.

AN UPGRADED RUNNER'S CLOSET

If you've got the basics covered and you're looking to kick things up a notch so that you can tackle more challenges or weather, or just feel extra badass, here are a few more of the pieces I've come to rely on heavily.

GUZZLE LIKE A MOUNTAIN WOMAN

Until we moved to Miami, I never considered carrying water on a run. Sure, I might need it, but ehhh, that sounded like extra work, which was not my MO. I quickly realized that by sipping on electrolytes a bit every mile, I could delay muscle cramps and even bonking! But I was still not convinced a hydration pack was necessary, so I stuck to my trusty handheld water bottle.

Handhelds can be a great option, but as I also learned they have a tendency to mess with your form. Simply due to the change in hand position, we often end up swinging that arm across the body, rather than continuing with the forward-and-back motion needed. Crossing the body twists our hips and wastes all kinds of energy.

Moving to Colorado where I started hitting the trails, I thought a hydration pack was suddenly a brilliant idea because I could bring snacks! Now, I love it for all my road running adventures too. There's a pocket for my phone, a place to stuff those running gloves once I'm warm, and nothing to mess with my form. You can find hydration packs or hydration vests in a variety of sizes, but for most road runners you won't need more than 2 liters for the bladder. After that, it's about looking for the features that matter most to you.

Do you want something supersmall and light? Do you want plenty of pockets for snacks, phones, tissues? Do you need one that fits a more petite frame? All of these are 100 percent available through most of the major pack carriers; head into a store to try on a few and get a feel for the fit.

DON'T LET IT RAIN ON YOUR PARADE

Similar to shunning cold-weather gear, I avoided the rain jacket purchase for ages as well, thinking it was extravagant. And maybe it is, to an extent because these jackets tend to be a little pricier to keep them both lightweight and water repellent. Yes, repellent as in, it will bead up, not resistant as in no water penetrates, because those jackets end up being like wearing a hot suit as your body heat is trapped inside.

But if having this extra piece of gear is one more way to bust your excuses to get out the door, then again it's worth every penny. Most often,

I've found that it's hardest to start running when it's already raining, but if it begins while you're already out there, it's no big deal. Try to keep that in mind and do your best to remember those days as a kid, where nothing was more thrilling than splashing in the puddles.

Speaking of puddles, once you're back inside post–rain shower, try stuffing newspaper in your shoes to help them dry out more quickly and retain their shape.

Get a Better Grip

Maybe you don't run trails, so trail shoes seem completely unnecessary, I get that. Until we moved to Colorado, I had a steady fourteen years of road- and treadmill-only running under my belt. I knew everyone seemed to love them, but it took me a bit of testing things out to find out not only how different trail running is, but what a pure joy it is.

Whether you hit the nature path or the paved path, trail shoes can be a fabulous option for winter running. They provide a little extra grip through the snow and are often better suited for the wetter conditions.

A much cheaper option, if you don't want to add to your shoe collection, is a pair of pull-on spikes for winter traction. They'll fit over almost any existing running shoe.

Listen Up

I'm starting to feel like a dinosaur as I tell you about how long I waited to buy things. But again, I thought, why shell out $150 for wireless earbuds when I have twenty-two pairs of headphones scattered about the house? You know, the ones where you have to figure out some clever way to wind the cord around an arm strap to keep it from flapping around or you end up holding it in your hand, all very efficient.

Wireless earbuds might be bonus gear, but they really are incredibly convenient. No more messing with wires, easily changing songs, plus hands-free calling. Now, what you listen to via those earbuds is a whole different topic and I'm going to touch on that in a minute.

A FANCY GPS WATCH

As the silver paper ripped to reveal the glorious green of my first Garmin Forerunner watch, I squealed with delight. This beautiful piece of technology felt like an exorbitant treat, a splurge, an I'm-not-sure-I-really-need-this kind of gift that, let's be honest, won my future husband major points for supporting my crazy. He continues to support it, which in turn makes him a little crazy, too.

But that watch, after years of mapping out my routes online, got me hooked on using technology to improve. Although I think many of the watches we all lust after have more functions than we genuinely need (I mean, very few of us run without our phone, which is a glorified computer), there are some that I really enjoy:

- Easy-to-see current pace
- Easy-to-set intervals for a workout
- Easy-to-track heart rate through the wrist strap
- Easy screen customization to look at our data

Honestly, that's the biggest chunk of what I have around. I could talk through sports bras and leggings, but you've got that handled, right?

OTHER AREAS TO SPLURGE OR SAVE

Social media is one of my favorite places to connect with other runners. Every day, I get to hear about runs that motivate me to show up in the winter and try new crazy trails or I get to ask questions to find out what's going on outside my running bubble.

The one big drawback is we also get to see every little thing that's being tried and tested. It leads to wondering whether we need to be doing all of these things to improve our running. In fact, I've gotten a few frantic messages from new runners who feel overwhelmed by the postrun wheatgrass-shot, cryotherapy-chamber, compression boot–wearing, cupping, honey-drizzled-face-mask routines they've been seeing.

Personally, I love to experiment. I'm fascinated by what I can learn about my body, what things work for me, and what things work for my friends but aren't my jam. Here's a rundown of some of the biggest things to help you decide whether they're worth your time, money, and energy.*

WHAT ABOUT VO$_2$MAX TESTING?

With GPS watches now showing a VO$_2$ number, I'm getting more questions about the necessity of a full-on test. Your VO$_2$max number shows the ability of your body to utilize oxygen and thus has been used as an indicator of endurance potential. As the number increases, it means you'll be able to perform at a higher level for longer (i.e., maintain your new goal race pace).

But is it accurate? Do you need to go mask yourself up and pay hundreds of dollars for a very uncomfortable treadmill run? Unless you totally geek out on data and information as I do, absolutely not. Very few runners are going to get a true benefit from this test. Especially as the data have now shown that having a high VO$_2$max doesn't necessarily translate to successful running.

The idea is that by testing to your absolute maximum, you can gauge total fitness and predict your endurance, while also creating heart rate zones for training. A simpler and cheaper method is to use perceived exertion to find your easy, moderate, and hard paces. Then, use your own running and racing to tell you how fit you are. It doesn't really matter what the test says.

The one piece of information that I do find useful, but you can get from a less intense metabolic efficiency test, is the heart rate crossover point where you go from burning predominantly fat as your fuel source to carbohydrates.

---

* If you'd like to skip this section, I'll simply say that, *no*, you don't need to do a single one of these things to be a runner. Some have more value than others.

WHAT ABOUT BLOODWORK OR DNA FITNESS TESTS?

Ahh yes, let us see your DNA and we shall tell you the future. Right now, DNA-for-fitness-recommendation tests are a bit like Magic 8 balls. Some of the advice will be spot on, such as you should eat more fruits and vegetables; others will be a combination of bizarre and confusing information.

After testing out a number of these on myself, I found that not a single one gave me workout information that was truly any different or more useful than what we all know to be true:

- Cardio is great for your heart and total health.
- Lifting weights is key to maintaining muscle mass and preventing imbalances that cause injuries.

Boom, saved you hundreds of dollars. If you are looking for more actionable information, I am a fan of bloodwork from such companies as InsideTracker. While it's in no way required to have a great season of racing, I am a firm believer it's an extremely valuable tool for distance runners. One quick peek at your blood could explain fatigue or ongoing injuries due to low vitamin D, high cortisol, or low iron stores, among a host of things. Bloodwork is a concrete way to see how your body is responding to training and nutrition, whereas DNA currently appears to be more generalized tips.

WHAT ABOUT CUPPING, NEEDLES, AND ALL THAT JAZZ?

Thank you, Michael Phelps, for introducing the ancient Chinese methodology of cupping to the world via the 2014 Olympics. In cupping, a glass cup is placed on your skin and then heated to create a suctionlike effect that pulls the skin up into the glass, with the idea that it will increase blood flow to relieve muscle tension, improve circulation, and reduce inflammation. I first tried this in 2007 on that inflamed IT band and I cannot tell you that it helped me in any way, but it wasn't the most unpleasant experience of my life, either.

If I were going to point you in the direction of something to help with pain, it would flow in this order:

- Chiropractor to ensure alignment
- Physical therapist to review movement patterns and prescribe strength exercises
- Massage therapist to help release tension (and because it freaking feels good)
- Acupuncture or dry needling to release muscle tension

WHAT ABOUT CRYOTHERAPY, COMPRESSION BOOTS, AND INFRARED SAUNAS?

Have you seen these Jetsons-like cylinders that fill with liquid nitrogen to lower the temperature to -240°F? You enjoy up to three minutes in this cold-therapy state, as an alternative to an ice bath. It's reported to help with inflammation, better sleep, mood boosting, and a whole host of other things.

Having tested it for thirty days, I can tell you that although it's interesting, the science doesn't yet prove it out and neither did my personal experience. Which is not to say that cryotherapy, or putting your legs in those compression boots that inflate and squeeze your muscles like a cobra, doesn't work! Any recovery that mentally makes you feel better is valuable and each of us will react differently, so test it out and give your body the love it deserves, to stay injury-free.

If you have the time and money to invest in consistently using a sports recovery center that can offer a variety of services, knock yourself out! It certainly isn't going to hurt.

But if you don't have access, then don't fret.

- Wear compression tights after long runs, to help recovery.
- Use heating pads (or the hot tub) to loosen tight muscles.
- Foam roll consistently.

- Put your legs up to drain fluid from them after hard workouts.
- Pay attention to total life stress, which impacts recovery.
- Focus on high-quality nutrition.
- Get a sports massage after big weeks.
- Replace your shoes before they're worn out.

WHAT ABOUT SUPPLEMENTS FROM PROTEIN TO GREENS?

A bevy of supplements are always being advertised to runners to help with joints, aches, energy, post workout, sleep, snot rockets, bedwetting, and so much more. It can quickly take a toll on both your wallet and your gut to keep pounding down more and more pills, powders, and magic creams. Which is why I'm here to help you sort through this whole mess, based on having been a guinea pig for many things to be able to tell you what works.

Overall, only a few things have made the cut long term:

- Turmeric: This has been an invaluable inflammation fighter and helped me recover well from my knee injury without needing pain meds.
- Plant-Based Protein Powder: Speaking as someone who struggles to eat enough protein for the miles I'm running, it's great to toss this into my green smoothie or have it with me when I travel as a better option than the bakery I'm drooling over.
- CBD Oil: My initial skepticism gave way after just a few weeks of consistent usage. Now, I'm a firm believer in this tool for fighting inflammation, improving sleep, and reducing those race day nerves.
- Oregano Oil Capsules: Anytime I travel and when I return home, these bacteria fighters are in my nightly routine and have kept me from the flu or a nasty cold for years.
- Digestive Enzymes and Probiotics: These just seem to do wonders for keeping my stomach working, which means my immune system stays stronger.

From there, you could get into things like beet powders and adaptogens, which all have their place, but aren't required for you to be your best runner self.

WHAT ABOUT PURCHASING A TREADMILL?

We now must talk about the elephant in the room. The one too often referred to as the dreadmill, which in no way is going to improve your enjoyment of using it. Buying a treadmill was one of the best investments I ever made in my running and, as of yet, the only downside I've found to runners' buying a treadmill is when they let it collect dust instead of utilizing it as a great tool.

Suddenly, I wasn't limited to the gym's forty-five-minute cap. Which simply meant stopping, looking around, and then restarting my treadmill because I was at Gold's Gym in Kansas City, where everyone else was busy hefting around barbells in their construction boots.

I didn't have to travel any farther than our house to get in my run when it was icy, when I had thirty minutes between phone calls, or when my knee was being weird and I didn't know how far I could go before I'd need to stop. It was my freedom to run as much or as little as I wanted. Other reasons to embrace the treadmill:

- No hazards to avoid, curbs to jump up and down, broken sidewalks, or cars
- Less impact with the cushioned belt
- Slight forward propulsion
- Add hills at any point in the run
- No track needed to measure distances for speed work
- Consistent pacing for intervals
- Feeling safe to run extra early or late
- Easier to focus on form and practice cadence
- Weather controlled in both summer and winter conditions

THE FREE 10%—MENTAL TRAINING

Putting aside all the dollar bills for gear is great, but there's one free area that you could be working on throughout training for maximum results. I've already told you about putting Margie in her place and there are some amazing books dedicated to sports psychology, so instead of poring over those details, I want to give you some actionable tools to use ASAP.

Mind games are bad in relationships, but great for running. Sometimes, you need to dial into how your body is feeling to ensure you're nailing that good running form, and other times, you need to find ways to stop your brain from focusing on why your left thigh suddenly has a weird twitch.

PUT ME IN, COACH

We often joke that running is 90 percent mental and 10 percent all the miles you put in during training. It's not quite that skewed, but the mental aspect is massive. Yet you won't find a single training plan where mental training is included as a workout.

As a coach, it's easier with one-to-one coaching to insert these types of tools because we know that each athlete requires something a little bit different. But every athlete needs the tools. So, if I were to attempt to break the molds and add mental training to a plan, it might look something like this:

Monday: Rest Day
Work on exploring your why for this race; find that deeper
     motivation.

Tuesday: Speed Work
Dynamic warm-up
1 mile easy
2 x speed play 3,2,1 with equal recovery

During the 1-minute push practice the mantra you want to use
for race day
1 mile easy cooldown

Wednesday: 7 miles easy
Gratitude miles

Thursday: 5 miles with last 10 minutes fast finish
Visualize that finish line feeling.

Friday: Restorative Yoga (all kinds of sneaky mental tools here)

Saturday: 3 miles easy
Practice embracing the feel of easy and not fearing going slow to
get stronger.

Sunday: Long Run
13 miles easy effort
Mentally embrace the hills, embrace the discomfort, lean into
knowing you're becoming a better runner.

As you can see, this gets awful wordy to put into a weekly table of workouts, and of course, that's without detailed strength and core workouts alongside the tips. Luckily, now you have the tools at your disposal to begin using ASAP for more joyful running and better racing.

CATCH THAT PURPLE SHIRT

In the final miles of a race, one of my favorite techniques has become to stop looking at the clock and start focusing on a racer in front of me. This was a useful tip provided by my husband during a race together where he kept pushing the final mile pace and I couldn't get my brain to quit yelling *stop!*

Find a very identifiable runner in front of you and make it your goal to catch him or her before the finish line. It takes the focus off how you feel and allows you to zone in on a much smaller goal. Of course, this is hard work, but it's more tangible to aim for that shirt than contemplate another mile of running.

To be clear, this isn't about catching them, turning around, and waving your fist in their face like *"aha, gotcha!"* Instead, it's about using the middle to pull us along and the momentum of our fellow runners to keep us pressing the gas pedal straight through the finish line.

JUST THE NEXT . . .

We've got 6 miles on tap for the day and maybe some of those miles are even supposed to be at race pace, but every step feels like a slog. This is when it becomes more important than ever to "run the mile you're in" as every cheesy coach has said to a runner at some point.

Breaking it down even further is the trick that gets new runners to surpass their perceived limits. It's not "I'm going to run 6 miles for the first time ever," it's just "I'm going to keep running to the next stop sign," and when that arrives, you pick a new feature in the distance and you only have to go that far.

Giving yourself repeated opportunities to stop if you've truly hit your breaking point, is a great way to ensure you don't feel that you've failed the workout. But also a sneaky way to convince yourself to go just a bit farther, because each time you reach a goal, there's a little dopamine boost that makes you think, "Maybe I could handle just one more block."

It's the same feeling you have when the finish line is in sight and suddenly your dead legs feel revived for a finishing push, and then after you cross, you've got plenty of energy to find the French toast that guy is eating and celebrate with your friends when, moments before, you were sure you couldn't take another step.

GRATITUDE MILES

We often talk about how running gives us space to think, but it's also really easy to turn on "This Is My Fight Song," zone out, and just do the work. Music is a fantastic tool on days when you might be challenging yourself at the track, but not always the best use of your time on easy runs.

A practice that I started with my athletes is called the gratitude mile, which becomes even more valuable as you begin increasing those long runs. You know, the runs where you start to question why you've chosen an endeavor that requires hours every Sunday. The runs where you lose feeling in your feet because they're so tired and yet you're fully aware of every single step. Those are the runs where learning how to implement a gratitude mile can mean the difference between quitting and finishing strong.

Gratitude miles can become a part of every single run or be reserved for one of those later miles. But as always, I think the more we practice it, the more we benefit from it. Especially if you're one of those runners (waves hands around like I just don't care) who swear they want to meditate, but don't. This is a version of that.

How to do it?

- Start your run however you normally would, with music or a podcast.
- Around mile 2 or 3, shut it down; that's right, silence.
- Give yourself some true quiet and tune in to your body.
- Take a second to check with your form, breathing, and heart rate, and just get a feel for the run without judgment.
- Insert gratitude.

For the duration of the next mile, mentally run through every part of your body that doesn't hurt and simply say thank you.

Thank you, big toe, for pushing off with strength. Thank you, shoulders, for being strong and relaxed. Thank you, core, for staying tight to keep me in good form. Thank you, driver, for not turning right on red and squishing me like the bugs on your windshield.

After you finish those, go on to everything else you can think of, from the ideas that pop into your mind most quickly or the last great hug you got, to the deeper feelings of security from having saved more this week. It can be anything and everything. As a morning runner, this has the bonus of starting the day with a better frame of mind.

How does this help you fall in love with training? It flips your perspective on hard runs. It reminds you that the miles aren't just about race day. It gives you a moment without Siri to find your own answers.

Become Someone Else

Labels are a tricky thing. When we say we have a sweet tooth, then it's impossible to turn down the postrun donut because that's simply who we are. When we say we're a runner, then it's much harder to skip our weekend long run because it's part of our identity.

Knowing this means you can put the concept of an alter ego or a specific label in place to achieve your goals. In *The Brave Athlete, Calm the F**k Down*, the authors talk about Beyoncé's choice to create Sasha Fierce as her on-stage presence when she first began performing. It allowed her to step out of any ideas she had of herself and perform with less fear because Sasha was a take-charge, go-big woman.

The idea is that you can embrace the same process to get over your race day fears, letting go of the worry that you aren't fast enough, or that this is just too hard. Since I've already got Margie dancing around my head yelling her negative thoughts, why not give her a friend: Fantasia Glitz.*

Fantasia shows up to races in the most brilliant, colorful outfits, strutting off the bus to the starting area like a woman who knows her place (right in the middle). Her huge smile is infectious and relaxes those

---

* This may or may not be from a "Find Your Stripper Name" meme because calling her Karen just didn't seem exciting enough and, well, Run To The Finish was my last creative naming attempt.

around her because she simply seems calm, in her element, and only slightly frozen, thanks to the two layers of throwaway clothes that make her look homeless.

Once the race starts, Fantasia carries this joyful attitude with her through the miles, remaining focused on being relaxed, taking in the moments, and knowing that she has more than enough inner drive to achieve anything she chooses. This is her day because every day is her day, even when it's not.

Now, more than anything, is when I wish books were interactive, because I'd love to hear what you come up with for your race day (or long run or track workout) alter-runner personality. The trick is to implement these great tools rather than skimming through this chapter and going right back to doing what you've always done. Which, I think we all know, means getting the results you've always gotten.

7 FEELINGS EVERY RUNNER HAS EXPERIENCED

1. Blah, blah, **boredom** when inactive friends tell you running ruined their knees, hip, back, insert ridiculous body part.

2. **Despair** when you realize that liar who said you were almost done wasn't even standing at the halfway point. Followed by murderous rage.

3. Smug **superiority** when posting your dark, cold early morning run before your friends even crawled out of bed. 'Cause that's how we roll.

4. Entirely **out of shape** climbing a set of stairs, even if you did run 10 miles over the weekend.

5. Complete **annoyance** when someone complains about their slow pace and it's better than your 100-meter sprint.

6. **Jubilation** at winning a race lottery; who needs those million-dollar tickets.

7. **Pride** at a running shoe collection to match every outfit. It isn't hoarding, it's practical.

CHAPTER 10

OWNING RACE DAY

Seven miles into my first marathon, I noticed my giant of a running partner was falling back. I slowed. He winced. I raised an eyebrow. He mumbled, "This isn't my day. My knee is killing me. You need to keep going without me, I can tell you're feeling good."

My brain exploded in a rush of fear and emotions. Was he nuts? We'd spent months doing long runs in the frigid Kansas City weather, with hidden water bottles that ended up partially frozen. This whole marathon nonsense was his idea. But I *was* feeling strong and very amped up on adrenaline, so after a bit more cajoling, I waved good-bye to his six foot five limping frame and started to pull away.

I laughed, giggled, and most definitely high-fived a few other runners over the coming miles. It was a freaking Disney movie in my mind, right up until mile 23, when I broke out into a full sob and wanted to quit on the spot. In retrospect, the fact that I hadn't taken in a lick of fuel almost entirely explains why my brain was prepared to shut down this seemingly arbitrary goal to run 26.2. But luckily, as with many things in my early twenties, it passed quickly and I was back on my way. The elation of what I was about to achieve carrying me onward.

With the finish line in sight, the joyful tears started again, and as I crossed, I knew deep down, *"I'll never do that again because I'm quite sure it isn't supposed to be that fun."* Although I did wait over two years to run my next marathon, breaking that vow, I can say that few of them have lived up to the joy of that first marathon because I became too wrapped up in goals over process as my measure of success.

In fact, after my eighth marathon I took a very long hiatus. Not from running. No, I continued to log the same number of miles annually, whether I had a race on the calendar or not, but I let go of the pressure because that time mattered to no one else. I had great adventures running through Iceland, running the Jerusalem Half Marathon, learning to run trails in Colorado and even at 12,000 feet in Jackson Hole, Wyoming.

When people ask me how I stay motivated without a race, I'm never quite sure what to say.

It's a habit.

It's a part of me.

It's a gift that I don't want to take for granted.

Since that marathon burnout, I've realized there is something magical about lining up, once we learn to get out of our head. Who's to say you're doing it wrong? That your race day goal, performance, or results weren't what they should be? For months now, you've focused on recapturing the joy of your runs and how embracing discomfort has made you more confident to conquer other big life goals.

Yet suddenly, on the starting line, clad in compression socks, surrounded by people you deem much faster, you've begun a spiral of what-ifs. Closely followed by a long inner monologue on why they're called butterflies; that sounds far too beautiful for what's sent you back to the Porta Potty line sixteen times.

---

* Jake also finished with the "I'll never do that again" thought and, true to his word, opted not to embrace that level of crazy once he'd crossed it off his bucket list.

Breathe. Once again, you're not alone. You don't have to lead the pack with a wiry, shorty short–wearing speedster clipping at your heels and attempting to derail your big goals. No. Instead, you're surrounded by thousands of other runners in exactly the same position of wanting to get the most from themselves today. You have the benefit of their energy to push you along, and when it gets really tough, you'll know you aren't alone.

The key difference between you and them is you know there's no wrong way to finish the race. The clock is telling but one minute of your very long, winding road to that start line. Let that reminder wash over you, and then it's time to control what you can for the best race possible.

DO WE EVEN NEED TO RACE?

Before discussing nerves and race planning, I think this is a fair question in a book that's all about asking you to break free from using your watch as a measurement of good and bad runs. Although racing for the clock isn't our primary goal, that doesn't mean you can't have a whole lot of fun by signing up for races, whether you want to parade around with thousands of other ladies dressed like princesses or gallivant through Antelope Canyon on a 55K trail race just because it's beautiful.

What I want for you is to find the joy in those days, rather than being so consumed by the need to hit a specific pace that you feel anything less is a failure. Training for months, learning about yourself, and dedicating yourself to the process is such a massive win, it shouldn't be diminished. I'm not anti–running for the clock because it can definitely push you to new levels, but I am anti-the-clock-determines-my-running-worth.

I used to feel compelled to have a race on the calendar. What runner doesn't initially? Every time you run, people ask what you're training for and it quickly feels like, without a race, there's no point in the miles. The problem was those races often interrupted my love of running because I got so nervous on race day that I usually underperformed and felt frustrated for weeks afterward. Which is a big part of why I now race when I want to and spend the rest of my year running tons of miles just because I can.

Over the years, I've found that I can race for fun, for a PR, or to test myself without letting those nerves dictate my day or how I feel about the results. Learning to harness those nerves is a key skill of longtime runners and, like most other things mentioned in this book, one that gets better with practice.

STEP 1: ALLOW YOUR TYPE-A PLANNER TO GO CRAZY

One thing most runners have in common is an ability to plan. It's the only way to make workouts happen amid the chaos of life and, of course, gives us a sense of deep satisfaction to cross things off a list. Preplanning for race day gives your brain something tangible to think about during taper and will eliminate unnecessary surprises.

Here are a few of the major points to plan:

- Plan how much time you'll actually need at the expo (it's never as fast as you think), parking, walking, checking out the free samples, and hopefully running into a few familiar faces.
- Check out the parking situation or know where you can be dropped off on race morning, to avoid the freak-out of sitting in traffic with the start time approaching.
- Review the weather to see if you need throwaway clothes at the start or will need something warm at the finish. Do *not* spend time freaking out about the weather; just be as prepared as possible.
- Select a specific spot for your spectators during and after the race. This ensures you have a better chance of spotting them on the course for a huge energy boost and eliminates wandering around in a fatigued state postrace.

- Set an alarm and a backup alarm to help reduce fears of missing one in the morning, which can leave you tossing and turning all night.
- If traveling, decide what your best options are for dinner the night before the race. Ideally, eat early, so you're back at the hotel and able to simply relax and wind down well before you need to sleep.
- If traveling, put your key gear in your carry-on. Nothing is worse than needing to run a race in brand-new head-to-toe gear.
- If traveling, pack your prerace food and double-check all your must-haves.
- The night before, lay out all your gear and pin on the race bib, so you're ready to go in the morning. No fumbling around in the dark; you've got your bagel with nut butter prepped and your preworkout mixed, no gear left behind.
- Eat your planned breakfast, even if nerves have banished your appetite. You'll need that energy in just a few hours.

Taper doesn't have to be the maddening, horrible time that we often portray on social media. I mean, the jokes are still funny and, much like being a bridezilla, you're given a grace period in the week preceding the race. Spending some of that free time planning, reviewing your training logs, and focusing on your mental preparation will help the time speed by.

STEP 2: WRAP YOUR NERVES IN A WARM BLANKET

Although none of us enjoys being nervous, once you start to reframe nerves as a tool for success, they can be a welcome reminder on race day that you actually care about achieving your goals. New studies have also shown that nerves prime your brain and get you focused on the task at hand.

Our goal is to harness that energy to propel us forward, rather than waste our mental energy before they finish singing the national anthem. Your job at the start line is to get in a little warm-up but otherwise conserve energy for the miles ahead. Stop bouncing around and chill out.

A few ways you can start to harness your nerves for a better performance:

- Recognize it as adrenaline and know it's a good thing; that's what pushes you just a bit harder than in training runs.
- Trust that once the race starts, you'll be ready to ride that extra energy boost.
- Stop focusing on the finish line and instead on each next step toward your goal. Finish the warm-up, run the first mile controlled, maintain your goal pace with each mile.
- Meditate. Okay, I know I said harness the nerves, but if you're ruminating all week on race day fears, then sitting down for a minute just to breathe is going to help you get a grip on what really matters. You may have trained hard, but it is just a race.

Now, of course, if nerves were all good, we wouldn't fret at all about those wonky little butterflies. Unfortunately, when you let your nerves start running the show, a bunch of not-so-great things happen.

- Elevated heart rate (means using carbs sooner in race)
- Wasted energy at the start line
- Disrupted sleep for multiple nights
- Mental fatigue before the race begins
- Altering our belief in what we can achieve
- GI distress (ugh, more time in the Porta Potties)

Being aware of these issues and how you can instead benefit from the adrenaline is part of taking control of your race day. It's also one of the reasons that practice races can be so helpful. They give us opportunities to test out what keeps us calm on days where we don't have a big goal on the line.

Practice races can be the same or shorter distance than your goal race. The focus is on learning what that start line feels like and how you can make it work for you. Followed by practicing effort management from start to finish, it's tricky to find that spot where you're pushing yourself harder than normal, but not so far you can't maintain it.

BE IN CONTROL

One famous lesson from those under heavy pressure (e.g., Navy SEALS and astronauts) is to control what you can in a stressful situation. This isn't a "forget the rest" situation, it's truly a mental feeling of taking control, which shifts your attitude.

Stop focusing on your watch or hitting a specific goal, and instead, start asking yourself, "How am I performing?" Aha, another big-picture process that will help you to get out of your head.

This means checking in on your form, your breathing, your fueling. Knowing that you have control over key areas of your performance is a reminder to actually pay attention to them. It allows you to assess whether this is not your day, without all the emotion around a time goal, either allowing you to pull back or to know that you can push harder without the mental fear holding you back.

KEEP IT IN PERSPECTIVE

Get a grip on what this race really means. Would a PR be great? Of course, that's an insanely great feeling to top off months of training! Are you still just as valuable as a person if you have an off day or don't run a certain time? *(Rhetorical, I hope.)*

This one tip alone makes such a difference for so many runners (finger point at myself) as it releases unnecessary pressure and often leads to better a race. Maybe for months, this has been *the* race in your mind, everything aimed at achieving your new personal best.

But then it's raining, you needed a Porta Potty stop, and you couldn't manage to weave over to the water table on the last aid station. It happens, and you're allowed to be frustrated afterward, but cap that pity party at 24 to 48 hours. Then, it's time to put it in perspective and start collecting all the best parts of the race to help you the next time around.

BE FASHIONABLY EARLY

Don't add to the craziness of race day by worrying that you might miss the start. Get there with enough time to hit the bathroom line, do your dynamic warm-up, and then relax. Seriously, relax.

Stop bouncing around and running a ton; get relaxed and save your energy. Wear throwaway clothes if it's cool. Again, conserve energy and reduce any mental strain; a tired brain needs more carbs. Although I genuinely hate being cold at the start line,* it's better than seeing a sea of red taillights in front of me and knowing that I waited too long and now will be praying in a mad dash from the car to the start line as runners are already on their way.

IMPLEMENT A ROUTINE

Have a routine that you do before every single run (a quick dynamic warm-up + same meal). This sets up your body and brain to be ready to run. It instantly provides a feeling of calm because you have performed this ritual before hundreds of runs.

A routine helps to prepare your mind and body for the workout ahead, which is why we're talking about things like your dynamic warm-up and not a ritual of putting on your left compression sock before your right. Although, if that mentally gives you a boost, by all means don't stray from the formula.

---

* In complete transparency, I only run a handful of races each year now. I run because I love it. But also, because I really dislike hanging around at the start line, so to all those races out there with the VIP section, yup, I'm in for those heaters and plush potties.

THINKING BIGGER THAN RACE DAY

A lot of folks have A, B, C goals. The idea is solid, but it can backfire when the race gets hard, because we stop shooting for A, knowing that B is also "good enough."

Instead, I like to have a Big Picture goal, as in what really matters to me most. For me, that's always loving the run and not getting injured. With those in mind, I'm going to push for that A goal unless it jeopardizes my long-term goals.

Now is a good time to say that DNF or DNS* are not dirty words. They are the choices that smart runners make, knowing that one race is not worth a debilitating injury or months off running because they chose to reach for a goal that wasn't really appropriate.

PICTURE YOUR FUTURE SELF

Wonder why the tip to visualize comes up over and over again in articles about elite runner preparations? Probably because it works. Much like clichés that seem too basic to pay attention to, they live on because they're accurate in their simplicity.

A few ways to do this during training:

- Generate the emotion you want to feel crossing the finish line as you finish each run.
- Imagine yourself throwing your hands up (not looking down at your watch) to get that stellar finish-line photo.
- See yourself hugging the first runner you pass to celebrate your achievement.
- Envision the words you'll say to those who've supported you in reaching that day.
- Dream of the luscious burger and sweet potato fries at your celebratory dinner where you'll be proudly sporting your race medal.

---

* *Did not finish* or *did not start* are the terms used for when you must drop out of a race or, as you may have surmised, when you don't even start.

Use this throughout training for maximum effect, but it's especially key during the final week of taper, when you're working to put those nerves aside. Give your brain a better idea to latch on to: victory.

RECALL THE WORST RUNS

Mentally review all the workouts you've put in, and especially the ones that were rough but you did them anyway. Remember that those hard days were followed by some great runs and that, some days, everything seemed like it should have been perfect, but was just off.

Alternatively, if you've had a less than stellar round of training, be honest enough in your review to say, "Okay, today is about having fun and not my initial PR goal." No one wants to downgrade a goal. It takes a lot of guts for you to be the runner that's smart enough not to push your limits, but instead to pull back and go race for pure fun.

STEP 3: STRATEGIZE TO WIN THE WAR

Now that we have a handle on your nerves, it's time to actually kick this race into gear with a plan. A strategy is also going to alleviate nerves, by taking away the need to make decisions in the midst of your brain being carb deprived: "I will go out at X pace in mile 1" keeps you from overshooting, which leads to crashing and burning later in the race. Or "I will get to the halfway point and, if I am still feeling strong, then start to push the pace more. If I still feel great at mile 10, then I'll pick it up again." These are your prerace decisions to keep you focused. Rather than just running with the pack or following a pacer who may be starting too fast, this goes back to my first point: be in control. Having these small pieces in mind will help you control the pace starting out and finish feeling strong, rather than clawing through because you got overzealous with that initial adrenaline boost.

What about using a pace group to alleviate nerves? I know you're tired of hearing me say that it all depends on you, but that's the truth.

PROS OF A PACE GROUP:

- You let go of checking your watch.
- You engage with others in the group or the leader, to help pass the time.
- It can hold you back from going out too fast.
- Pace group leaders are often fabulous cheerleaders.

Many times, you'll have a chance to meet your pace group leader at the race expo. Use that opportunity to see whether this person might be the added boost you need to blaze through that new PR. Things to ask pacers include their most recent race times; find out whether this is an easy time for them to hit. Ask whether they chat or how they like to encourage the group. Ask what their pacing strategy is and how they handle water stops.

A supercommon issue for many runners is to find the pace group whizzes through the water stop, whereas they're used to stopping, walking, and sipping. Then, they dash off in a sprint to catch the group . . . and a few rounds of this sucks up all their energy!

CONS OF A PACE GROUP:

- You might feel crowded in a group that won't spread out.
- Not all pacers are equal; some are used to running much faster and have trouble reining it in.
- Even pacers have bad days or don't feel well.
- Their pacing strategy may not be best for you (e.g., starting fast).
- It can feel defeating if you aren't hitting their pace right away.

Personally, I hate the bustle and bump and grind of being tightly packed around someone carrying a stick. Instead, I tend to run on my own, but keep an eye out for the pacers. This is a good way to notice whether I've gotten ahead of my goal finish time or I'm falling off.

Now that we've done the planning, let's examine a few more ways to make your race day the best possible.

8 OTHER MISTAKES TO RUIN YOUR RACE

Ask experienced runners for their best race day tips and it almost always includes "Don't start too fast" and "Don't try anything new on race day."

While those two are critically important, they skip over a whole host of other mistakes that we've all blocked out and then don't relay them to you. Unless you prefer to learn things the hard way, here are eight mistakes to avoid for a great race.

MISTAKE 1: BIG PRERACE DINNER

Let's start with what we do the night before the race, which can derail us. In the most simplistic terms, stop signing up for the all-you-can-eat pasta dinner. It's usually too much food, too much fat, and not the way you normally eat.

Overeating means all that food can make you feel sluggish in the morning or impair sleep as your body works to digest things it's unaccustomed to. Stick to what you've had during training, which could indeed be your Friday night slice of pizza, and avoid being one of the statistics:

> More marathons are won or lost in the porta-
> toilets than they are at the marathon . . .
>
> —Bill Rodgers

MISTAKE 2: NOT FULLY THINKING THROUGH RACE DAY CLOTHING

Shoulders hunched, squatted down to wrap my arms around my bare legs, I realized that Las Vegas at four a.m. is much, much colder than I'd anticipated. In fact, I could see my breath and was wasting loads of energy shivering, muttering curses, and bouncing around to stay warm. Entering the starting corral, I noticed discarded hats, gloves, and scarves, which I promptly picked up and put on because it was worth the risk of lice to stop the madness.

That was the last time I ever forgot to bring throwaway clothes to a start line. Save yourself the misery and conserve your energy by learning from my faux pas. Head to Salvation Army for some items if you don't have anything in your closet that you've been meaning to donate anyway.

With that mistake out of the way, it's also important not to overdress and leave yourself with too much gear to handle during the race.

- Avoid tying anything around your waist; the extra material will become frustrating as the miles progress and you begin to fatigue.
- Pick up a cheap pair of gloves that you can toss midway through the race if you start to warm up. Alternatively, wear your wicking gloves and plan to stick them in your waistband.
- Garbage bags are an easy way to keep warm and repel water if it's raining at the start line and you want to feel dry for a bit longer. For truly wet days, consider putting duct tape on the front of your shoes to keep out water and prevent blisters.
- Double-check anything with zippers to ensure it won't rub or bother you on race day.

MISTAKE 3: UNDERESTIMATING CHAFING

On normal days, a little antichafe skin lubricant on your thighs probably does the trick, but on race day, it's time to nearly bathe in the stuff. Your gait and stride often change later in the race due to the new levels of fatigue, which can mean a sudden rubbing on your big toe or along your sports bra straps.

Clothing may also become more wet than normal from sweat, which again enhances the potential for friction. These two factors make it critical to lubricate toes, heels, legs, underarms, around the waistband, and men, get those nipples. Male runners often find it's necessary to wear

Band-Aids for additional protection (*an awkward Band-Aid is way better than a bloody shirt*).

MISTAKE 4: SKIPPING ELECTROLYTES

Hydrate, hydrate, hydrate. We've all heard the never-ending stories about how performance declines with dehydration, but equally important is keeping electrolytes balanced.

Options include taking something like SaltStick prior to the race (especially great option for hot races or heavy sweaters) or alternating each water stop with sports drink and water. Beyond that, don't feel compelled to guzzle down a full cup at every aid station. Keep sipping consistently and then rehydrate well at the finish line.

MISTAKE 5: IGNORING PRE- AND POSTRACE FUEL

Nerves and adrenaline often cause many to feel a little queasy, or at the very least, absolutely not hungry on race morning. Skipping breakfast puts you at a disadvantage before you even cross the starting line.

Because training runs are often done at a lower intensity, the body relies more on fat stores than readily available carbohydrates, allowing many runners to skip prerun fuel during training and yet bonk on race day without it. If you start the race in a carb-depleted state the feared bonk is much more likely to happen.

Bananas are a great option for settling an upset stomach and happen to be a great prerace source of fuel. Topped with a little nut butter, it's an option that works for many.

Postrace, runners once again find themselves easily skipping food as their hunger levels are generally overshadowed by fatigue.

However, the body needs to be replenished to ensure you start the recovery process and can of course fully bask in the joy of what you've just done! Try just getting a few bites of whatever is available, along with an electrolyte drink . . . maybe not so much the donuts or cookies. Save the fun for the celebration meal.

MISTAKE 6: CLOCK WATCHING

While we often have a PR goal in mind, I've found that by focusing on how we feel instead of the watch, we often run a better race.

You might PR unexpectedly because you don't hold yourself back or you might run a slower race, but know that you did your best because it was all the effort you had available.

MISTAKE 7: NOT ASKING FAMILY FOR SUPPORT

We often feel that training itself takes up enough time that we shouldn't ask for anything more. But, consistently, I hear (and have experienced) my athletes say that nothing gave them a bigger boost than coming upon a friend, husband, or child during the race. Whether you stop for a hug or just know they're there rooting you on, it puts some extra oomph in your step when you might be ready to slow down.

MISTAKE 8: NOT PREPPING MENTALLY

Knowing in advance that you will have hard moments makes them easier to manage. Suddenly, they're an expected and very normal part of your race, rather than a moment to let Margie take over and lead you down a wormhole of doubts.

RACE DAY ETIQUETTE

Racing is inherently a solo activity. Only you can control your speed, your mind, and your pain threshold. Sure, you're surrounded by thousands of other spandex-clad runners, but you aren't so much working together as simply forging ahead with lips pursed and eyes laser-beamed on the person in front of you.

So, if we're out there for ourselves, is there race etiquette to be followed? Not the ask–Miss Manners, white-glove, no-snot-rockets kind, but yes.

After months of training, everyone arrives at the start line a little amped up, anxious, and determined. Maybe that means shuffling a little closer to the front; maybe it means nerves that require a few more bathroom breaks; maybe it means music loud enough to drown out the negative voices.

It always means thousands of people focused on their own goals, but needing to flow together for optimal enjoyment and performance.

Whether you're fearful of lining up at your first race or your britches have gotten too big from being a longtime runner, here are a few fun reminders to make everyone's experience more fun and, hopefully, PR worthy.

RACE SHIRT

DO feel free to wear it on race day for something like a Halloween run or a Pink event.

DON'T wear it for longer distances; it's an unspoken rule of "earning" the shirt.

DO wear the race shirt from the previous year if you ran to show off your veteran status.

DON'T wear race shirts from races you didn't run.

BATHROOM BREAKS

DO use the provided Porta Potties.

DON'T judge those who have to use a bush because lines are too long.

DO bring your own toilet paper to the start.

DON'T, seriously, just don't, leave the Porta Potty so gross even a desperate runner won't use it.

START LINE

DO get in your assigned corral. They have them to prevent people from getting run over as well as to prevent faster runners from being slowed down.

DON'T wear your bib on your back; this is not a rodeo.

DO feed off the energy of those around you and line up with friends.

DON'T run 5 wide and make it impossible for anyone to pass your merry band.

FINISH LINE

DO run all the way across both mats to get your time and best photo.

DON'T get cranky with the volunteers. You might be tired, but they are unpaid help making our enjoyment possible.

DO encourage any runner you are passing with a very simple "good job" or "we got this."

DON'T assume you know why someone is walking or tell that person to run.

BANDIT

DO run a few steps if a friend really needs you, unless the course is already supercrowded.

DON'T hop in right after the start and hop off right before the finish. Race directors will tell you they plan support for a certain number of runners and, of course, most races benefit a charity, so you're cheating them, too.

WATER STOPS

DO begin moving to the side of the water station when you see it coming up, to avoid sprinting horizontally through traffic.

DON'T come to a complete stop, unless you like being shoved from behind.

DO slow down and walk, if needed, just keep moving forward.

DON'T take Gatorade at every stop (your stomach will thank you).

TRASH

DO toss your cup to the side.

DON'T drop it in the middle of the road for everyone else to run over (it becomes slippery).

DO look before you toss, to avoid sloshing volunteers or other racers.

DON'T treat the street like a garbage can. Hold on to those gel wrappers until you see a trash area.

WALK BREAKS

DO move to the side.

DON'T be afraid to take them, whether it's your race plan or just a must-stop-now-before-I-die feeling.

DO look behind you to avoid slamming into someone as you move to the side.

DON'T stop midstride in the middle of the road.

And I feel that it goes without saying, but no cutting the course short! We've seen a lot of reports of this lately, and it sucks for everyone involved. You'll get blacklisted and the people who really earned a spot on the podium will be cheated and you didn't earn it, so really, how good will it make you feel?

NAIL THE RACE PHOTO

And since we're all about having more fun, what if you could actually get a decent race photo? With Brightroom saying its average purchase rate is around 5 percent, I know I'm not alone in uttering the following after spending a week excitedly waiting to see whether its photographers finally snapped a stellar image:

I swear I was running not walking.

Surely, I don't look like that while I run.
Maybe it's just a bad angle.

Improve Your Form

If ever there was a time to check in on your form, this is it. Stand up tall, pick up those knees, and get those arms pumping forward and back. Consider the photographers your personal on-course coaches; they'll give you a little boost each time you smile and pull yourself together.

Be Camera Aware

Just like scanning for your friends and family, keep your eyes peeled to the roadsides for photographers, often in neon safety vests. Running to the side of the road, rather than up the middle, can be a good way to ensure that you're snapped. But do that only if you feel best there! I'd rather get a good staged photo than throw off the whole race for a chance at one itty moment.

Once you see the camera, plaster on that smile and remember why you love running. Even if you're hating every step in that moment, trust me, after the finish line when you're ready to sign up again, you'll need that photo as proof to friends and family that you really do enjoy this.

Finish Line Flair

We all want to know our finish time immediately, but assume you took an extra ten seconds to stop your watch after running all the way through the finish line, arms stretched out in victory. If you start to slow before crossing that very last mat, you'll get walking photos, which is superfrustrating after busting your hump. In fact, don't just run through, let all those emotions come flooding out! Smiles, cheers, jumps, yells, tears . . . you'll get a second look from the photographers and just think you might get one of those spectators excited enough to register for their own race.

Race day often feels momentous because we describe it as the culmination of all our hard work. But really, it's just one more finish line that brings us to a new starting line, and releasing some of the power around it can make racing far more enjoyable. Interestingly, many runners find that when they let go of the clock or the fears, they have their biggest PRs. Likely because all their energy was focused on running and not wasted in a tightened face or worry about failing.

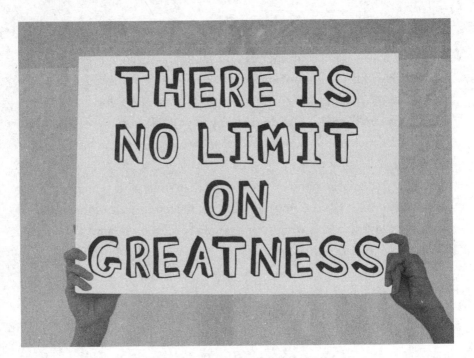

HOW TO SPOT A RUNNER ON SOCIAL MEDIA

You needn't worry; we'll tell you that we run. But here are a few sure-fire signs you've found yourself a runner.

1. The gratuitous postrun watch photo

2. A sweaty selfie holding up fingers to indicate miles

3. The top-down selfie looking at our snazzy running shoes

4. The fake "I'm tying my shoe" photo

5. Clothes laid out on a bed with a bib for our flat runner

6. A standing leg stretch, which we honestly only did for the photo

7. Recovery photo wearing compression socks and holding a mug of coffee

CHAPTER 11

DEVELOPING A LASTING PR

After the fanfare, the blaring music, rushing through the corrals to find your family for a very sweaty hug and maybe some tears, you waddle home and kick up your feet. There are a few days of processing how everything went, then it starts to hit you that training is done. Your goal is behind you and if you wanted to continue lying on that couch all week, all month, all year, it wouldn't hurt anyone's feelings.

Nonsense; get up and get going.

Whether you had the best race of your life or one of the many that don't go as planned, each finish line is simply a new starting line. Poetic? No, just an annoying bit of optimism to remind you that we're on this journey for so much more than a finish line result.

Close your eyes for just a moment and think of three things you learned during this round of training. Maybe you realized that winter running can be cathartic as you escape the stuffy indoors. Maybe you found that on days when you skipped your morning workout, you were less productive and a bit more, shall we say, unpleasant in stressful moments. Maybe you found that allowing yourself walk breaks made the whole process more enjoyable and perhaps that lesson flowed over into your to-do list.

Running can be whatever you need it to be: A respite from the insanity of your constantly chirping phone. A place to challenge yourself in ways you otherwise can't throughout your day. A calm meditative movement through the repetition. Or merely an excuse to suck in some fresh air and feel the sunshine on your face.

Whether you choose to chase a new time or distance goal, doesn't matter. Now, you've found the real key to running is simply moving forward. Each step carrying you to a better version of yourself.

It's amazing how something we do so freely as children may become less appealing as we age. And yet, can serve as a little beacon of light letting us know there's more out there waiting if we dare to take the journey. It's not bad for our knees. It's a proven mood enhancer. And mostly free. My twenty-two pairs of running shoes would disagree, but on the whole, I can run anywhere, anytime, just by lacing up.

Now, the real goal is to find ways to carry this spark of joy with you. As Marie Kondo says, this means getting rid of the clutter. When you find yourself teetering on the edge of burnout or losing motivation, it's the time for a deep scrub around the edges and a big black trash bag to toss out the mental crud that no longer brings you joy.

HOW TO AVOID BURNOUT

Over the 21,000 miles I've now run, there have certainly been moments of feeling "over it." Usually at the finish line of a marathon that didn't go quite as planned, but on the whole, there's simply nothing like running to bring me satisfaction. Learning to avoid burnout is a big part of what's kept me running consistently for almost two decades, that and the dynamic warm-up.

Burnout, not to be confused with overtraining, though the two often happen simultaneously, usually rears its head as a serious case of our inner terrible twos screaming "*but I don't wanna*" every time we're supposed to lace up.

If left unchecked, you give in because who can resist a crying baby forever? You skip a run and it feels kind of fantastic to give your body some rest. Then another run, which makes you feel guilty, but not as guilty as the couch feels good. Then, you've excused multiple long runs and suddenly it's marathon weekend and you're left wishing you'd applied a little tough love.

Burnout is a condition that has physical, emotional, and psychological aspects. Burnout is real; it leads to fatigue, loss of motivation, depression, and even anger. Although overtraining can feel similar, it's usually a physical sensation of having truly pushed too far and your mind wanting to continue when your body is saying no.

As someone who has run nearly the same annual mileage for a decade, I can tell you that burnout isn't necessary. It's supernormal to have periods of feeling fatigued during the marathon training buildup, which can border on burnout. But a few little tricks of the mind and the training can keep you running with a smile much longer.*

GIVE YOURSELF A BREAK

Sometimes burnout is a direct result of type-A tendencies. Needing to follow the plan to a T, nailing every workout, and of course, focusing on that massive PR attempt can lead to unnecessary stress. Why place the entire focus of your running on the outcome of one day?

Matt Fitzgerald discusses the idea of fun leading to improvement in *RUN*: "Prioritizing enjoyment and trusting that the more fun we have in training, the fitter we will become." I think this is because it allows us to be flexible with our training and releases the performance pressure because no matter the finish line result, we've enjoyed the journey.

---

* Maybe you're thinking, "Who is she kidding, I never have the energy left to smile on a run." In which case I'm talking about the metaphorical smile of your soul. But also, remember that science has proven smiling during your workout can make it feel easier!

With flexibility, you recognize when you need an extra rest day or understand how to really slow down for a useful recovery run. You don't feel the need to push every run just a little harder than you should.

GIVE THAT STARTING LINE A SECOND CHANCE

In complete contrast to the last tactic is to jump into a 5K or 10K race in the next couple of weeks. Many runners get reinvigorated to train hard through a little extra competition, and often from the surprising results that show they're making progress. It's harder to stay motivated for the sixteen to twenty-four weeks it takes to reach marathon race day, so having these small checkpoints can help you with an adrenaline boost and the pure fun of being surrounded by other runners.

Can't find a local race? You might get the same benefits from a virtual race or from simply hopping into a group run every few weeks. So many prefer solo run time that I'm not suggesting you must have a running group. However, when you're feeling a little less motivated, these are the runs that will take your mind off the pace and often push you a tad harder on speed workouts.

Important note here: if you're feeling fatigued, worn out, or on the brink of injury, be smart enough *not* to employ this tactic.

EXPLORE OTHER MOVEMENTS

It goes without saying that one way to get over running doldrums is simply to stop running. Do something else, from Pilates to rock climbing, for a day or even a week. Often, a few days of moving your body in new ways or slowing down with yoga will leave you jonesing for a run. (Ask any runner who has ever been injured!)

At a minimum, it will give your muscles a break so you come back with fresher legs, and who doesn't love it when a run feels easier? Give your body a chance to absorb all the work you've been putting in over the last few months and your mind an opportunity to miss the endorphins. It's easy to begin taking what we once loved for granted, when it's become such a standard part of our routine. Let go of any guilt over missed mileage or lower monthly totals and allow yourself to enjoy those other workouts. In an unexpected twist, a lot of runners often fall in love with other workouts, such as swimming or CrossFit, and end up becoming better runners!

KNOW THAT, ONCE AGAIN, YOU'RE VERY NORMAL

Even the most talented, dedicated, hard-core athletes experience burnout.

Find comfort in knowing that nearly every runner has moments of doubt at some point in weeks 12 to 16 of an 18-week cycle. Misery loves company and all that, but more important, you know that this feeling will pass for you, just as it has for all those who trained before you.

I don't always feel like washing the dishes or cleaning the sheets, but I do like the lack of bugs and disgustingness in my home, so I continue anyway. At times, you'll need to continue anyway, to hit your goal. But if it drags on for weeks and weeks, then it's time to evaluate whether this goal is worth losing the joy of your workouts.

SLOW DOWN. WAY DOWN.

Do you get caught up in the numbers on your watch, instead of focusing on how each week of training is designed to build upon the previous week? Feeling that a slow run is a sign that you're going backward rather than toward that shiny new race pace? There's going to be accumulated fatigue and then built-in recovery with every good training plan; your biggest job is to learn to trust the slow.

One easy way to start reining in your easy runs is to stop looking at your pace and start focusing on keeping your heart rate and perceived exertion low. Know that in those long lower-heart-rate runs, you're teaching your body to use fat, allowing yourself to increase your total running volume, and building a more powerful aerobic engine for distance running.

Matt Fitzgerald dedicated an entire book, *80/20*, to showcasing all the studies that prove that doing 80 percent of our runs at an easy pace is the best way to get to a race day PR. Elite runners naturally use this strategy through their 120-mile weeks, but we middle-of-the-packers tend to believe we need to cram more into our shorter-mileage weeks. Incorrect.

Most of the time, we need more miles on our legs and to have a little more fun in the process of training. Slowing down means more chats with friends, getting in another podcast episode of *Dr. Death*, or just an extra few minutes away from the craziness of your life. Embrace the slow.

REMEMBER THE ADVENTURE

Remember this entire experience is an adventure. Not just the times you get to runsplore in a new city, but the little moments in every run where you have that glimpse of yourself that's surprising: *"Who knew I could run that far?!" "Can't believe I pushed through that one." "Something in my body doesn't feel right."*

Focusing on the entire journey makes each run more important and more enjoyable. You'll often hear elite runners say that every run should have a purpose, and you might initially think that means form or speed or endurance. But sometimes, the purpose of a run is freedom, relaxation, community, or exploration. When your singular focus is race day, the individual runs lose importance and thus desire declines. Adventure can also mean changing up your running.

- Find new paths in your neighborhood or, *gasp*, drive somewhere new.
- Seek out a Rave Run. Remember those features in *Runner's World*? Although I love the simplicity of running out my front door, sometimes it's worth the effort to turn your run into an experience.
- Make a goal for each run before you start, to help remember the importance of each one.
- Take it off the roads once in a while for a little vitamin Nature boost.
- Run your normal route going the opposite direction.
- Volunteer at a race to get excited by the determination of other runners.

- Include a shorter race in part of your long run for the day.
- Throw in some walk breaks or little pickups to change the feel of your run.

REMEMBER REAL-LIFE HUMAN CONNECTIONS

Solo running is one of my great joys. It's that time where I can freely think about the world or choose not to think about anything at all! But when you're nearing burnout, sometimes the best solution is not to give yourself hours alone in your head, thinking about how every muscle hurts and wondering why you ever thought this was a good goal.

Maybe it's a run with a friend that knows you well enough to bring Hot Tamales for your long-run fuel, as a special pick-me-up. Maybe it's seeking an entirely new crew to help you break out of a rut. Maybe it's just calling that one friend you keep meaning to catch up with and picking a spot to meet. Not only will the miles pass through your chatter, but you'll have someone along who understands exactly how you're feeling.

It's hard to complain to the nonrunners in your life about burnout because they'll often say, "You're doing too much." Whereas a fellow runner will dive in with questions like how's your sleep, your fuel, your life stress? And then give you their personal and very honest assessment that you need to cut yourself some slack or that it sounds as if you're in the midst of some serious runner growth and you need to just hang on a bit longer.

Just remember that your group should be supporting you, not pushing you so hard that every workout becomes a race. This is unfortunately supercommon for those who run with a group multiple times per week, which can mean you're not getting in enough easy runs, and that can definitely lead to injury and burnout.

REIGNITE THE JOY?

One of the unintended side effects of being injured is that you realize just how important running has become in your life. Most runners will hold on to that feeling for a month or so after returning, but it's possible to keep it going for many years if you spend a little time on each run simply remembering why you love it.

Take the time to not just do your workouts, but keep your mind engaged and excited about the process of training.

- Check out Pinterest boards for motivation.
- Scroll those Instagram #motivationmonday quotes.
- Review your training logs as a reminder of how much you've achieved.
- Look at race medals to conjure up those special feelings.
- Acknowledge that without the really bad runs, you'd never appreciate the ones that leave you feeling like a million bucks.

It's not unusual to see me post on social media that I freaking love running. Mostly as a reminder to myself that I'm choosing this, but also because the second I say it, the grin on my face is nearly unstoppable and my readers respond that it helped them to go out and have a better run. Running just isn't that serious from the middle of the pack, which gives us all more freedom to enjoy every mile we get.

Long Run–Only Goodies

It might sound strange, but put aside a few things that you're only allowed to use or have on long runs. I *love* the feeling of being able to go all day from a preworkout, but I save it specifically for long runs. It's my secret mental boost to make the run better and it happens to taste good.

Perhaps for you, it's Sour Patch Kids or the one day you allow yourself a froyo date with the family. While I know rewarding ourselves with food is taboo, I'm not talking about the idea that you burned 2,000 calories, so you should now binge on burgers and fries for the rest of the week. This is about finding the little things that are going to give you a mental edge on the run. For many, that's the postrun donut or beer with their crew, whereas I'm dreaming of lounging in an Epsom salt bath with a good book.

I also have audiobooks that I save for long runs because it makes me think all week about getting back out there to find out what happens next. It's a bonus that gets me excited to spend a few hours on my feet.*

INSTAGRAM, HASHTAG, TWEET IT

Head down, pushing ahead, we often miss the beauty of the areas we're running through. Under normal circumstances I would say put that cell phone away, but oddly in this one instance, thinking about a photo to share from the run forces you to connect with where you are.

Once you've posted, add a few hashtags like #RunToTheFinish, #RunChat, or #WeRunSocial and watch the running/fitness community show up to be your cheerleader. On bad runs, they help remind you it will pass, and on great ones, they give you a virtual high five.

Social media can get a bad rap because of the comparison trap. But the community that I've found there is second to none. It excites me to try new races, to push my boundaries, or to embrace my rest days because all the smart people are doing it, too.

What I want for you more than anything is not to need a PR to enjoy your runs. Celebrate the heck out of every single new record that you achieve, but remember you can have hundreds and thousands of great runs that never involve crushing the clock.

POSTRACE RECOVERY PLAN

Maybe you aren't burned out, but are in that space after a big race where you don't know what to do with your tired body and excess energy. Everyone, myself included, is telling you to give your legs some rest, but you

---

* Over the last few years, I've read and listened to more than a hundred books a year. So, yes, for me this is a huge motivator because I love stories, but especially stories about running while I'm running. If Rich Roll can do five Ironmans back to back, then I can probably figure out how to go just one more mile.

feel jazzed from the achievement or burning to get at it because the day didn't go as planned.

Plus, you have an endless loop of *"Will I lose fitness by taking weeks off after my marathon?"* flitting through your mind and making you do less-than-smart things, such as trying to run.

It's a concern for nearly every runner I've encountered in the months postmarathon where we're battling the postrace blues, attempting to run on legs that feel like cinder blocks, and craving those runner endorphins.

Did you know that most elite runners take off at least a month post-marathon? I love these two thoughts from *Meb for Mortals*, because I fully agree:

- Most runners should be able to take off at least 3 weeks without any loss in fitness gains.
- Don't allow this to become a break in your training, just a shift.

They don't expect to maintain peak fitness year-round, and neither should you. I've now compared you to elite runners multiple times in this chapter and you're silently thinking, "I am not an elite, what they do doesn't apply to me." I understand, but hear me out. Yes, they log more miles or race at a higher level, but what you're doing is the same thing. A build of mileage and intensity, crescendoing with a massive performance and now your body, while possibly not as compact as theirs, needs to be treated to the same level of recovery if you want to keep running without injury.

Being on the same page, I now want to help you get through those weeks postrace to not lose the gains you've made, reclaim your motivation without that massive race goal, and keep running strong.

Your first big advantage is the schedule you've kept for months of training. Allow yourself to slide back into that routine. Get up at the same time. Exercise at the same time you used to run. Maybe it's a walk, mobility, yoga, or foam rolling, but keeping the habit alive will make it easier to cross-train consistently and come back to running when ready.

Why do we need time off after a race?

Recovery is important for both the novice and elite runner because the toll of 26.2 miles on the body is just the same regardless of finishing time.

A study in the *Journal of Neurological Sciences* showed that it takes a minimum of **14 days for muscle inflammation to decrease** and return to full power; other studies have proven it can **compromise the immune system for the same period of time**. During training, especially peak week, you're pushing your body to its limits and it responds by adding some adrenaline to keep you going, which suppresses the immune system and helps you power through.

Once you begin taper, the immune system goes into overdrive, ready to kick out anything that looks like an illness. That means you're more susceptible to illnesses that are going around (especially when you hop on that plane to travel to the race!). It's also why you might get sick in the days after a race.

In fact, according to David Nieman, professor of health and exercise science at Appalachian State University, someone running the Western States 100-miler has a 1 in 4 chance of getting ill. Aha, now that really smart people have told you running too soon could cause either injury or illness, which will then mean you need to take even more time off, let's just assume that you're going to be supersmart and not overdo things.*

Here's a proven postrace recovery plan to get you from walking backward down the stairs to walking fully upright and running pain-free soon.

Immediately Postrace

Begin refueling with whatever food your body can tolerate, but ideally an electrolyte drink to replenish sodium, magnesium, and zinc, along with a high-quality carbohydrate and protein. Often the easiest choice is a green smoothie, until hunger fully sets in later that day, as discussed in Chapter 8.

---

* Many of my running friends who do multiple marathons per year will shorten the recovery period. But even the elites don't do that, so be smart with your choices and not swayed by what others are doing.

- Carbohydrates: Your muscles are primed to replace depleted glycogen, which will speed recovery, so grab that banana or head out for your celebratory pancakes.
- Water: Most of us are not able to maintain complete hydration throughout the race, so start sipping and keep sipping. Don't feel compelled to guzzle, as this could lead to an upset stomach.
- Keep Moving: Try not to stop and sit right away; the slow walk through the finishers' chute is good to keep your legs from seizing up.
- Ice or Epsom Salts Bath: Studies go both ways on this. I prefer a nice hot Epsom salts bath to loosen muscles, but an ice bath can be great after hot races. Choose the one that is most relaxing to you.

ONE DAY POSTRACE

Get in some movement to loosen up your muscles. Consider getting a light massage to encourage blood flow to the muscles, which along with compression will help speed up recovery or at least help you stop walking like a penguin. Do not get a deep tissue massage that will only further inflame the muscles. Save those massages for high points in training where you need extra help working through muscle tightness.

Continue to focus on enjoying high-quality anti-inflammatory foods. It doesn't mean you can't enjoy any treat meals, but the more greens, veggies, and quality proteins you ingest, the quicker your body will repair. If you are feeling a lot of soreness, consider using turmeric capsules in place of an over-the-counter medicine.

- Sleep: You've heard it before, but sleep is one of the best recovery tools available. If you are traveling and having trouble, consider taking melatonin (a natural hormone).
- Compression: I'm a *huge* fan of compression for recovery. It simply increases blood flow to the area, which promotes recovery.
- Heat or Ice: If you're having pain, use ice for swelling and heat for tightness. That's right; you have the green light to skip the ice bath if you hate it, and head to the hot tub.

TWO TO THREE DAYS AFTER

Keep the movement easy with some walks or restorative yoga. This time is all about slowing down, to relish in the culmination of months of work and treating your body well.

Even if you are beginning to feel better, **resist the urge to run**. Your muscles have more microscopic tears than you realize and the added rest will help ensure you don't jump back too quickly, which could lead to injury.

If you're getting an eye twitch thinking about more rest days, then now is when you can start to ponder adding in active recovery. Don't get too excited; you are not yet heading out to a HIIT class or scaling tall buildings. Instead, we're thinking low-impact workouts that are going to help with both recovery and your running when you start back up.

Active recovery benefits runners in several important aspects:

- It **minimizes the buildup of lactic acid** in the muscles, which is responsible for stiffness and soreness in the days following a tough workout.
- It helps **lower your heart rate**. Athletes whose bodies recover more quickly to a resting heart rate level enjoy improved endurance over time.
- It **improves mobility and flexibility** with workouts you'd other-wise skip entirely.
- It **maintains a habit.** This is one of the things I love most about not just sitting for the day. Instead, you get going at your standard workout time, maintaining the link in your brain that this is when you do sweaty things.

This could include things like walking to explore the place you trav-eled to for the race, renting a cruiser bike to also explore that area, swim-ming easy laps or just lounging in saltwater for extra healing benefits from the salt, a restorative yoga class, or mobility workout. If you didn't travel for the race, then just get outside in your own city or neighborhood and spend some time moving with those who've missed you during the previous long weekends dedicated to training.

FOUR TO SIX DAYS AFTER

Continue with the active recovery, but if you're starting to feel better, you could add light cross-training. This isn't the time to head to your first CrossFit class, no matter how good you might be feeling, but you could do a little longer bike session, swim workout, or a standard yoga flow. This is also a good opportunity to schedule a deeper massage to flush out your muscles and break up any adhesions for the following week.

You'll be hitting the time limit for whether friends and family want to hear about your magnificent feat. Make sure you relive it one more time to get in all the details, all the emotions, and are 100 percent convinced they know you are phenomenal.

SEVEN TO THIRTEEN DAYS AFTER

Let your body be your guide to exercise, but keep the intensity low—and only run if nothing hurts. **All runs should be done at a very easy, relaxed pace.** Yes, I bolded that to ensure you would not only read it, but possibly read it twice and commit it to memory.

Week 2 postrace, you're feeling energized again, but notice that when you attempt to run, your legs often won't cooperate. This is a good sign they're still working through the muscle tears and trauma of being pushed past previous limits. Give them a break and put that energy to work on the cross-training, which as previously stated, will make you a better runner. Get going with the upper body, core work, and perhaps mobility.

Most runners will find that the longer they have been running, the sooner they can resume running because their muscles are used to hard efforts. Which is why it may seem like I'm over here telling you knock it off and rest your legs, when you see a friend out hitting the pavement just days after a race. Let me once again turn to science for some extra wisdom on the matter.

Researchers from the Ball State University Human Performance Laboratory compared a group that didn't run for a week after their race, with a matched group that ran easily for 20 to 40 minutes a day. The nonrunners scored better in tests for muscle strength and endurance ten days after the marathon.

From additional athlete studies, they found it takes your muscles and skeletal system from seven to ten days to recover, with some biopsy research showing muscle-fiber damage still lingering thirty days after a marathon. Beyond that, your stress hormones and other body functions are out of whack from the extreme bodily stress, so instead of worrying about getting in a run, it's time to focus on optimizing your health.

SAMPLE RECOVERY WEEK

You've had a plan for months and I can tell are already feeling lost without one to follow. Thus, I've put together a very simple little list to help guide you through your first week of active recovery, along with details about why each type of workout is recommended during this phase.

Monday: Restorative yoga and a little walk
Tuesday: Walk and more restorative yoga
Wednesday: Walk and upper-body weights/core work
Thursday: Walk or bike and Vinyasa yoga
Friday: Walk and Pilates
Saturday: Walk or bike and yoga
Sunday: Easy 1- to 2-mile run and walk

WHAT IS RESTORATIVE YOGA?

It's usually the nemesis of runners who prefer to be moving quickly and working up a sweat. However, it's a great tool that can be used throughout training and in particular during the first week postrace to help the body settle back into alignment and release tightness without overstretching or overexerting the muscles.

The following are a few restorative poses that help to release a tight low back and de-stress the entire body:

- Legs Against Wall: Performed with a bolster under your legs, hips, or back
- Supported Child's Pose: Sitting on your knees, press backward so you are folded over your legs with a bolster under your chest.
- Reclining Bound Angle: Lie on your back with your knees bent and feet together, then allow your knees to fall out to the side.
- Hip Release: Lie on your back in corpse pose (fully relaxed, all limbs straight) and place a block under your hips.

WHY ALL THE WALKING?

Complete rest after a race can cause a body to feel stiff and tight. My friend, it's time for you to embrace the joy of walking, slowing down to take in the neighborhood you might otherwise quickly pass through.

Too many runners turn up their nose at walking, thinking it's only something you do once you've slammed headfirst into the dreaded wall. Instead it's time to realize you could reap some major endurance benefits from slowing down.

- Walking builds endurance (consider it extra credit training).
- It utilizes the same muscles without the impact.
- Walking eases low back pain (an issue of many desk jockeys).
- Walking strengthens your feet.
- Walking large hills strengthens the glutes without the heart rate raising intensity.

All those benefits mean that once your legs are feeling better and your mind is ready to go, you'll have an advantage because you didn't simply sit around for a few weeks. You literally took steps that will make you a better runner.

HOLDING ON FOR THE LONG HAUL

You've followed the recovery plan and started adding a few runs back, but how do you keep the spark alive? How do you wind up on the front porch with a head full of gray hair, not talking about races gone by, but races still to come?

It's everything we've talked about in this book. Finding your why. Embracing the good and the bad runs for what they are. Allowing yourself to run for the pure joy of the freedom it brings. Taking in the lessons that it teaches us and knowing there's so much more ahead if we're willing to continue showing up.

It doesn't matter if you walk. It doesn't matter if you never get one second faster. It doesn't even matter if you don't always reach the finish line of every race. Because that finish line is just a new beginning and you're offered that spectacular opportunity each time you lace up.

All that matters is the decision to keep moving forward, one step at a time. May we run long, healthy, and to the finish.

BONUS

After seventy thousand plus words, you'd think I've covered everything there is to say about loving your run and doing it injury-free, but I would beg to differ. Which is lucky for me because it means I remain employed with so much more to write, and lucky for you because it means bonus resources!

If you're looking for additional laughter at our chosen recreation, videos on how to work your hips and glutes, or tips on fueling the perfect race, head on over to http://www.runtothefinish.com/bonuses.

And, of course, if you're in the market for a running community, you know where to find me and the other run lovers on social media with #RunToTheFinish or shoot me a message on any of the platforms where I'm regularly chatting:

https://instagram.com/runtothefinish
https://facebook.com/runtothefinish

FUNNY RUNNING QUOTES

There's nothing like a great motivational quote to get you out the door, but that's far too serious to end this book. Instead, I leave you with some of my favorite funny running quotes.

Some people don't have the guts for distance racing. The polite term for them is sprinters.
—author unknown

The trouble with jogging is that, by the time you realize you're not in shape for it, it's too far to walk back.
—Franklin P. Jones

I've got 99 problems, so I went on a run to ignore them all.
—unknown

I don't believe in jogging. It extends your life—but by exactly the amount of time you spend jogging.
—Marshall Brickman

Good things come slow—especially in distance running.
—Bill Dellinger

They say good things take time; that's why I run slow.
—ME!

ACKNOWLEDGMENTS

First, to my husband. The man with no social media accounts, who hates to write and doesn't understand a single bit of my job, but unconditionally has supported me through it over the last decade. There's no one I'd rather run beside or laugh with, and that's the greatest gift of all.

To my parents, who never once allowed me to believe I couldn't do something if I was willing to work really hard at it. Who gave me the freedom to be the independent, strong-willed child that I was and, while also not understanding a lick of my online work, continued to be my cheerleaders.

Finally, to you dear readers and friends. I started RunToTheFinish .com in 2007 as a way to connect with other runners because I didn't have them in my daily life, and that is exactly what happened. It's grown and changed over the years to include other social media platforms, but each day, I'm blown away by the inspiration, motivation, friendship, and connection that we so easily find with runners around the world.

Here's to many years of finding one another on the roads with a nod and shuffling along to our BQ by 80 goals.

RESOURCES

CHAPTER 2

Noel E. Brick, Megan J. McElhinney, and Richard S. Metcalfe, *Psychology of Sport and Exercise*, January 2018: "Periodic smiling may improve movement economy during vigorous intensity running. In contrast, frowning may increase both effort perception and activation." Runners were 2.78 percent more efficient when smiling than frowning, reducing their perceived rate of exertion.

Susan Davis-Ali has a PhD in social psychology from the University of Michigan and currently serves as chief social science consultant to AnitaB.org and president of Leadhership1, LLC. Quoted from Suzanne Brue, *The 8 Colors of Fitness* (Delrey Beach, FL: Oakledge Press, 2008).

The Blue Zones: 9 Lessons for Living Longer from the People Who've Lived the Longest, by Dan Buettner (Washington, DC: National Geographic, 2009), provides additional reminders that while our runs are great, we need to be active throughout the day and embrace our crazy runner community.

CHAPTER 3

Carrie Cheadle injured athletes quote is from an *Outside Online* article about returning from injury: https://www.outsideonline.com/2184916/how-mentally-come-back-injury.

CHAPTER 4

G. H. Lo, J. B. Driban, A. M. Kriska, T. E. McAlindon, R. B. Souza, N. J. Petersen, K. L. Storti, C. B. Eaton, M. C. Hochberg, R. D. Jackson, C. Kent

Kwoh, M. C. Nevitt, and M. E. Suarez-Almazor, "History of Running
    Is Not Associated with Higher Risk of Symptomatic Knee Osteoarthritis:
    A Cross-Sectional Study from the Osteoarthritis Initiative," *Arthritis Care
    RES* 69, no. 2 (February 2017): 183–191.
R. S. Deane, J. W. Chow, M. D. Tillman, et al., "Effects of Hip Flexor Training
    on Sprint, Shuttle Run, and Vertical Jump Performance," *Journal of Strength
    and Conditioning Research* 19, no. 3 (September 2005): 615–621, reported
    the 9 percent improvement due to hip strength.
The 180 stride rate was initially reported in G. A. Cavagna, F. P. Saibene, and
    R. Margaria, "Mechanical Work in Running," *Applied Physiology* 19, no. 2
    (1964).

CHAPTER 5

According to FindMyMarathon.com statistics, there were approximately
    502,000 marathon finishers in the United States and Canada in 2018,
    which accounts for less than 1 percent of the adult population.

CHAPTER 6

A German study by Peter Limbach and Florian Sonnenburg, financial ex-
    perts from Karlsruhe Institute of Technology and the University of Co-
    logne, published by the Social Science Research Network, showed that
    CEOs who run marathons lead companies that are valued 4 to 10 percent
    higher than those run by nonrunning CEOs, https://www.researchgate.net
    /publication/272303335_CEO_Fitness_and_Firm_Value.

CHAPTER 7

A. P. Jung, "The Impact of Resistance Training on Distance Running Perfor-
    mance," *Sports Medicine* 33, no. 7 (2003): 539–552.

CHAPTER 8

D. Aune, P. Giovannucci, P. Boffetta, L. Fadnes, N. Keum, T. Norat, D. C.
    Greenwood, E. Riboli, L. J. Vatten, and S. Tonstad, "Fruit and Vegeta-
    ble Intake and the Risk of Cardiovascular Disease, Total Cancer and All-
    Cause Mortality: A Systematic Review and Dose Response Meta-analysis
    of Prospective Studies," *International Journal of Epidemiology* 46, no. 3 (June
    1, 2017): 1029–1056, published online February 22, 2017, doi: 10.1093/ije
    /dyw319.
Douglas Paddon-Jones and Blake B. Rasmussen, "Dietary Protein Recommen-
    dations and the Prevention of Sarcopenia: Protein, Amino Acid Metabolism

and Therapy," *A Current Opinion in Clinical Nutrition and Metabolic Care* 12, no. 1 (January 2009): 86–90, doi: 10.1097/MCO.0b013e32831cef8b.

Cheri D. Mah, Kenneth E. Mah, Eric J. Kezirian, and William C. Dement, "The Effects of Sleep Extension on the Athletic Performance of Collegiate Basketball Players," *Sleep* 34, no. 7 (July 2011): 943–950.

Sara B. Seidelmann, Brian Claggett, Susan Cheng, Mir Henglin, Amil Shah, Lyn M. Steffen, Aaron R. Folsom, Eric B. Rimm, Walter C. Willett, and Scott D. Solomon, "Dietary Carbohydrate Intake and Mortality: A Prospective Cohort Study and Meta-analysis," *Lancet Public Health* 3, no. 9 (August 2018): e419–e428.

CHAPTER 9

L. Malisoux, J. Ramesh, R. Mann, R. Seil, A. Urhausen, and D. Theisen, "Can Parallel Use of Different Running Shoes Decrease Running-Related Injury Risk," *Scandinavian Journal of Medicine and Science in Sports* 25, no. 1 (February 2015) 110–115, doi: 10.1111/sms.12154.

CHAPTER 11

Robert S. Hikida, Robert S. Staron, Fredrick C. Hagerman, William M. Sherman, and David L. Costill, "Muscle Fiber Necrosis Associated with Human Marathon Runners," *Journal of the Neurological Sciences* 59, no. 2 (May 1983): 185–203.

INDEX

Training. *See also* Mental training;
    Solid training; Training
    plans (*continued*)
    rest days, 106
    timelines, for races, 94–95
    visualization exercises, 215
    workout details, 131–132
Training plans. *See also* Marathon
    training plans
    Half Marathon Beginner Plan,
    123–124
    Half Marathon Intermediate
    Plan, 125–126
Trash, during races, 224
Treadmills, 10, 21, 198
Triceps dip, 151
Turmeric, 197, 240
Twisting while running, 74
Type A personalities, 52, 231

U

Ultrarunners, 10
Urgent care centers, 55

V

Veganism, 176
Vegetables
    eating more, ideas for, 163–164,
    180–181
    fighting hunger with, 157
Visualization, 215
Vitamin deficiencies, 165
VO$_2$max testing, 194

W

Walking

for postrace recovery, 244
during a race, 47, 224
during runs, 10
run-walk method, 7, 48
run-walk training plan–
    Galloway method, 113–115
during warm-up, 141
while injured, 121
Wall press activation, 79
Warm-ups. *See also* Dynamic
    warm-ups
    extending, 58
Watches
    checking time during races, 221
    GPS watch, 189, 193
Water, 46, 191, 240
Water stops, 223–224
Weather, on race day, 210
Weight gain, 101, 162
Weight lifting. *See* Strength training
*What I Talk About When I Talk About
    Running* (Murakami), 14
Whole foods, 171–174
Wicking gloves, 188, 219
Winfrey, Oprah, 10–11
Winter running, 188
Wireless earbuds, 192
Workouts. *See* Body-weight
    workouts; Cross-training;
    Speed workouts; Training

Y

Yasso, Bart, 19
Yoga, 145, 243–244

Z

Zinc, 239